Unit Assessment

McGraw Hill Education

Bothell, WA • Chicago, IL • Columbus, OH • New York, NY

www.mheonline.com/readingwonders

Send all inquiries to:
McGraw-Hill Education
Two Penn Plaza
New York, New York 10121

Printed in the United States of America.

6 7 8 9 10 11 12 QVS 18 17 16 15 14
D

The McGraw-Hill Companies

Table of Contents

Teacher Introduction

Unit Assessment

Unit Assessment is an integral part of the complete assessment program aligned with ***McGraw-Hill Reading Wonders*** and the Common Core State Standards (CCSS).

Purpose of *Unit Assessment*

Unit Assessment reports on the outcome of student learning. As students complete each unit of the reading program, they will be assessed on their understanding of key instructional content. The results of ***Unit Assessment*** serve as a summative assessment by providing a status of current achievement in relation to student progress through the CCSS-aligned curriculum. The results of the assessments can be used to inform subsequent instruction, aid in making leveling and grouping decisions, and point toward areas in need of reteaching or remediation.

Focus of *Unit Assessment*

Unit Assessment focuses on key areas of English Language Arts as identified by the CCSS—comprehension of literature and informational text, vocabulary acquisition and use, command of the conventions of the English language, and writing within the parameters of specific text types.

Administering *Unit Assessment*

Each unit assessment should be administered once the instruction for the specific unit is completed. Make copies of the unit assessment for the class. You will need one copy of the Answer Key page that features the scoring table for each student taking the assessment. This table provides a place to list student scores. The data from each unit assessment charts student progress and underscores strengths and weaknesses.

NOTE: Due to time constraints, you may wish to administer the unit assessment over multiple days. For example, students can complete Questions 1–40 on the first day and address the writing prompt on another. If you decide to break-up administration by assessment sections, please remember to withhold those sections of the test students are not completing to ensure test validity.

After each student has a copy of the assessment, provide a version of the following directions:

Say: *Write your name and the date on the question pages for this assessment.* (When students are finished, continue with the directions.) *In the first part of the test, you will read three selections and answer questions about them. In the next part of the test, you will read drafts and/or passages. You will revise these for clarity or edit for the correct grammar, mechanics, and usage. In the final part of the test, you will read a prompt and write a response. Read each part of the test carefully. For multiple-choice items, completely fill in the circle next to the correct answer. For constructed response items, write your response on the lines provided. For the writing prompt, plan your writing on the lines provided and craft your final version on another sheet of paper. When you have completed the assessment, put your pencil down and turn the pages over. You may begin now.*

Answer procedural questions during the assessment, but do not provide any assistance on the items or selections. Have extra paper on hand for students to use for their responses to the prompt. After the class has completed the assessment, ask students to verify that their names and the date are written on the necessary pages.

Overview of *Unit Assessment*

- Students will read three selections in each assessment and respond to items focusing on Comprehension Skills, Literary Elements, Text Features, and Vocabulary Strategies. These items assess the ability to access meaning from the text and demonstrate understanding of unknown and multiple-meaning words and phrases.
- Students will then read a draft that requires corrections or clarifications to its use of the conventions of English language and/or complete a cloze passage that requires correct usage identification.
- Students are then presented with a writing prompt that asks them to craft a response following the expectations of a particular text type.

Reading Selections

Each unit assessment features three "Cold Read" selections on which the comprehension and vocabulary assessment items are based. These selections reflect the unit theme to support the focus of the classroom instruction. Selections increase in complexity as the school year progresses to mirror the rigor of reading materials students encounter in the classroom.

Comprehension—Multiple-Choice Items

Comprehension items in each unit assess student understanding of the text through the use of the Comprehension Skills, Literary Elements, and Text Features that were the focus of each unit's instruction.

Comprehension—Constructed Response/Performance Task

A total of six items in each unit assess student understanding of the text by having them craft a written response to a question/prompt. Four of the items are short response items that assess student comprehension of the text using Comprehension Skills, Literary Elements, and Text Features. These items feature six lines on which students can write their responses. Two of the items are extended response, performance task items. One item requires student interaction with multiple texts; the other requires focus on a particular text. These items feature a page of lines on which students can write their responses.

Vocabulary—Multiple-Choice Items

Vocabulary items in each unit ask students to demonstrate the ability to uncover the meanings of unknown and multiple-meaning words and phrases using the Vocabulary Strategies that were the focus of each unit's instruction.

English Language Conventions/Grammar, Mechanics, Usage—Multiple-Choice Items

A total of ten items in each unit ask students to demonstrate their command of the conventions of standard English. Students are required to correct errors and clarify writing by editing/revising existing drafts or completing cloze passages.

Writing—Writing Prompt

Students craft a written response to a prompt in a previously-taught text type––Narrative, Informational, or Opinion. This activity assesses students' ability to write on demand in response to a prompt and is consistent with the writing performance students encounter in high-stakes testing. Students use the lines provided to plan their writing and compose their final version on a separate sheet of paper.

Scoring *Unit Assessment*

Questions 1–40 constitute a fifty-point test.

Multiple-choice items are worth one point each; short response items are worth two points; and extended response items are worth four points. For written responses, use the correct response parameters provided in the Answer Key and the scoring rubrics listed below to assign a score. Responses that show a complete lack of understanding or are left blank should be given a *0*.

Short Response Score: 2

The response is well-crafted and concise and shows a thorough understanding of the underlying skill. Appropriate text evidence is used to answer the question.

Short Response Score: 1

The response shows partial understanding of the underlying skill. Text evidence is featured, though examples are too general.

Extended Response Score: 4

- The student understands the question/prompt and responds suitably using the appropriate text evidence from the selection or selections.
- The response is an acceptably complete answer to the question/prompt.
- The organization of the response is meaningful.
- The response stays on-topic; ideas are linked to one another with effective transitions.
- The response has correct spelling, grammar, usage, and mechanics.

Extended Response Score: 3

- The student understands the question/prompt and responds suitably using the appropriate text evidence from the selection or selections.
- The response is a somewhat complete answer to the question/prompt.
- The organization of the response is somewhat meaningful.
- The response maintains focus; ideas are linked to one another.
- The response has occasional errors in spelling, grammar, usage, and mechanics.

Extended Response Score: 2

- The student has partial understanding of the question/prompt and uses some text evidence.
- The response is an incomplete answer to the question/prompt.
- The organization of the response is weak.
- The writing is careless; contains extraneous information and ineffective transitions.
- The response requires effort to read easily.
- The response has noticeable errors in spelling, grammar, usage, and mechanics.

Extended Response Score: 1

- The student has minimal understanding of the question/prompt and uses little to no appropriate text evidence.
- The response is a barely acceptable answer to the question/prompt.
- The response lacks organization.
- The writing is erratic with little focus; ideas are not connected to each other.
- The response is difficult to follow.
- The response has frequent errors in spelling, grammar, usage, and mechanics.

Scoring *Unit Assessment*

The Writing Prompt should be scored using the rubric found below.

4-Point Scoring Rubric

	Focus	Organization	Support	Conventions
4	Consistent focus is maintained throughout the writing.	Writing employs an appropriate organizational strategy that is followed throughout.	Writing is clearly supported by specific details. The word choice is precise and engaging.	Writing contains few, if any, errors in the conventions of standard English.
3	Consistent focus is maintained for the most part.	Writing employs an organizational strategy, with occasional digressions.	Writing has supporting details and the word choice serves the purpose of the writing but is not very precise.	Writing contains some errors in the conventions of standard English.
2	Writing loses focus at times.	Writing attempts to use an organizational strategy but it is not clear or consistent.	Writing has few supporting details and the word choice is often simple or unclear.	Writing contains several errors in the conventions of standard English.
1	Writing does not have a consistent focus.	Writing has no organizational strategy.	Writing has a lack of supporting details and the word choice is limited.	Writing contains serious errors in the conventions of standard English.

Unscorable responses are unrelated to the topic, illegible, or contain little or no writing.

Evaluating *Unit Assessment* Scores

The goal of each unit assessment is to evaluate student mastery of previously-taught material. The expectation is for students to score 80% or higher on the assessment as a whole. Within this score, the expectation is for students

- to correctly answer more than 9 of the multiple-choice comprehension items;
- to score "2" on short response items and "3" or higher on extended response items;
- to correctly answer more than 7 of the multiple-choice vocabulary items;
- to correctly answer more than 7 of the multiple-choice items assessing conventions of standard English; and
- to score "3" or higher on their written response to the prompt using the 4-Point Rubric.

For students who do not meet these benchmarks, assign appropriate lessons from the Tier 2 online PDFs. Refer to the unit "Summative Assessment" spreads in the Teacher's Editions of ***McGraw-Hill Reading Wonders*** for specific lessons.

The Answer Keys in ***Unit Assessment*** have been constructed to provide the information you need to aid your understanding of student performance, as well as individualized instructional and intervention needs.

This column lists the instructional content from the unit that is assessed in each item.

Question	Correct Answer	Content Focus	CCSS	Complexity

This column lists the CCSS alignment for each assessment item.

This column lists the Depth of Knowledge associated with each item.

23	B	Main Idea and Key Details	RI.5.2	DOK 2
24	I	Context Clues	L.5.4a	DOK 2
25	A	Prefix *re-*	L.5.4b	DOK 1
26	see below	Main Idea and Key Details	RI.5.2	DOK 2

Correct answer parameters for the constructed response items are found after the scoring table.

Comprehension: Multiple-Choice 1, 6, 8, 12, 14, 16–19, 21, 24–26, 28	/14	%
Comprehension: Constructed Response 9, 10, 20, 23, 29, 30	/16	%
Vocabulary 2–5, 7, 11, 13, 15, 22, 27	/10	%
Grammar, Mechanics, Usage 31–40	/10	%
Total Unit Assessment Score	/50	%

Scoring rows identify items by assessment focus and item type and allow for quick record keeping.

Read the next two articles. Then answer the questions that follow.

Sailing the Seas

Put together wood and canvas. Power them with wind. What do you get? You have created the sailing ship. For thousands of years, the sailing ship was the principal means of ocean travel. Early explorers used their knowledge of astronomy to guide them as they traveled on sailing ships to visit other lands and map the world. People used sailing ships to trade with other countries. People settling new lands also traveled across the oceans on sailing ships.

Beginning in the 1840s, a new type of ship began to sail the seas. It was called a clipper ship. Clipper ships were among the most beautiful sailing vessels ever built. They had long, narrow bodies and tall masts to hold their many sails. When the wind filled their sails, clipper ships seemed to fly across the water.

Clipper ships were built to be faster than other sailing ships. Before clipper ships, it could take 200 days to travel from New York to California. Clipper ships could make the trip in less than 100 days.

Shipbuilders competed to build the fastest clipper ships. The finest designer and builder of clipper ships was Donald McKay, who learned to build ships when he was in the navy and then ran a shipyard in Massachusetts. Between the launching of his first ship in 1845 and the closing of his shipyard in 1873, McKay built some of the largest and fastest clipper ships. One of McKay's ships, the *Flying Cloud*, set a record for the fastest trip from New York to California. In 1854, it made the trip in 86 days.

GO ON →

Clipper ships were used to transport goods around the world. They carried tea and silk from China to New York and California. Clippers also moved goods produced on the East Coast to gold miners and settlers in California. The cargo on a clipper ship was valuable. One clipper ship, the *Challenger*, returned from China carrying silk and tea worth $2 million.

In the 1860s, new forms of transportation began to replace the clipper ship. Railroads were built across the United States so people could use trains to ship goods. Steamships were also invented. Steamships had a big advantage over clipper ships and other sailing ships. They did not have to depend on wind for the power to propel them. They had engines powered by steam. Steamships could run in a greater variety of weather conditions, so they were more reliable than clipper ships. Then, as now, traders wanted to beat their competitors. They wanted to arrive at their destinations before anyone else and with the most cargo. So, of course, they turned to steam-powered vessels. In a short time, the age of the sailing ship had ended.

GO ON →

Fulton's Triumph

A nervous crowd moved about on a dock on the East River in New York City on August 17, 1807. Robert Fulton was set to make a trip up the Hudson River to Albany and had chosen several brave friends to go with him. It would be the first trip of its kind on a boat powered by a steam engine.

When the boat was being built, Fulton often noticed people making fun of it and joking about it. The boat was big—about 150 feet long—but it didn't look like other ships of the time. It was only 13 feet wide, and it had just one small sail and a flat bottom. A large paddle wheel stuck out on both sides. People thought it was misnamed the *North River* and should have been called *Fulton's Folly* because it was so foolish.

When it was time to begin the trip, Fulton's friends looked worried. Things did not get better when the *North River* stopped moving only a short way from the dock. Some of the passengers grumbled and wished they had not come.

Fulton was able to fix the problem with a minor adjustment. Soon the boat was rapidly moving up the river. It made its first stop at the town of Clermont. Later, people gave the boat the name of the town, *Clermont*. It traveled the first 110 miles in just 24 hours. Fulton reported passing many schooners so quickly that they seemed as if they were anchored. In another eight hours, the boat arrived in Albany.

The passengers gladly left the boat for dry land. They were thankful they had made it safely. Still, they told Fulton he probably couldn't do it again. Even if he could, they thought it would be unimportant to people.

Fulton posted a sign seeking passengers for the return trip to New York. He would charge $3, the same price as the sailing ships. Only two passengers signed up. Most people were afraid the steam boiler would explode. The crew fed a roaring fire with pine logs. The tall chimney spouted a dense stream of black smoke and steady shower of sparks. One observer thought the boat looked like a sawmill mounted on a flat-bottomed boat and set on fire.

GO ON →

The steamboat looked very different from the silent, majestic sailing ships of the time, especially at night. The crews of some sailing ships thought it was a monster racing down the river. They hid below the deck when it passed. Other people stood on the banks, waving handkerchiefs and cheering in celebration.

Fulton and his passengers arrived back in New York City safely. The boat had covered 300 miles in 62 hours, a little more than 2½ days. Sailing ships traveled the same route in about seven days. Gradually, people became less frightened, and Fulton's business grew. People were willing to pay high prices for the quick trip on the Hudson. Land travel was slow and uncomfortable. Shifting winds and tides made sailing the river unpredictable. Within a year, Fulton's company was earning $1,000 a week, and Fulton soon became one of the richest people in the country.

Fulton and others improved the design of the steamboats and made them more comfortable for passengers. One steamboat towed barges that contained sleeping rooms. Before, people had slept above the boilers. With this new boat, passengers could sleep well away from the dangers of the fire.

Within 15 years of Fulton's first voyage, at least 69 steamboats were churning up and down the Mississippi and Ohio Rivers. About 15 years after that, new steamships were designed to undertake ocean voyages. Fulton did not invent the steamboat, but he made it an economic success. Today, his first boat might be called *Fulton's Triumph* rather than *Fulton's Folly*.

GO ON →

Name: ______________________ Date: ________

Use "Sailing the Seas" on pages 1 and 2 to answer Numbers 1–10.

1. Read these sentences from the article.

   Steamships had a big advantage over clipper ships and other sailing ships. They did not have to depend on wind for the power to propel them.

   What does *propel* mean in the sentences above?

   Ⓐ stop

   Ⓑ guide

   Ⓒ move forward

   Ⓓ search for shelter

2. Read this sentence from the article.

   Early explorers used their knowledge of astronomy to guide them as they traveled on sailing ships to visit other lands and map the world.

   The word *astronomy* is based on a Greek root meaning "star." What does the word *astronomy* mean?

   Ⓕ study of the stars
   Ⓗ space travel

   Ⓖ making maps
   Ⓘ building ships

3. Read this sentence from the article.

   Then, as now, traders wanted to beat their competitors.

   Which definition fits *beat* in the sentence above?

   Ⓐ to mix by stirring

   Ⓑ to defeat in a contest

   Ⓒ to shape by hammering

   Ⓓ to pound into a powder

GO ON →

Name: ______________________________ Date: __________

4 What information from the article supports the idea that Donald McKay was the finest designer and builder of clipper ships?

Ⓕ One of McKay's ships set a record for the fastest trip between New York and California.

Ⓖ McKay learned to build ships when he was in the navy.

Ⓗ McKay built ships between 1845 and 1873.

Ⓘ McKay ran a shipyard in Massachusetts.

5 How does the author explain the end of the age of the sailing ship?

Ⓐ by comparing sailing ships to railroads

Ⓑ by describing a sequence of events in transportation

Ⓒ by listing the problems caused by clipper ships and their solutions

Ⓓ by describing what caused people to turn to new forms of transportation

6 Look at the illustration on page 2. What can you learn about clipper ships from the illustration?

Ⓕ They did not carry passengers.

Ⓖ They were larger than other ships.

Ⓗ They had smaller crews than other ships.

Ⓘ They had several main masts and many sails.

GO ON →

Name: ______________________ Date: ________

7. How does the author help the reader understand the great popularity of clipper ships?

Ⓐ by explaining the value of their cargo

Ⓑ by describing their beautiful appearance

Ⓒ by showing how they affected travel time

Ⓓ by listing the places in the world they transported cargo

8. Based on the article, what is the author's view of clipper ships? Use clear text evidence to show how the author supports this view.

____

____

____

____

____

____

GO ON →

Name: ______________________________ Date: __________

9 Read these sentences from the article.

Then, as now, traders wanted to beat their competitors. They wanted to arrive at their destinations before anyone else and with the most cargo. So, of course, they turned to steam-powered vessels. In a short time, the age of the sailing ship had ended.

What point does the author make about traders who turned to steam-powered vessels? Use clear text evidence from the article to support your response.

____

____

____

____

____

____

10 The author explains both the development of clipper ships and their replacement by steam-powered ships as a result of the same cause. From information in the article, explain the reason for the development of clipper ships. Use clear text evidence with details from the article to support your answer.

____

____

____

____

____

____

GO ON →

Name: ______________________ Date: ________

Use "Fulton's Triumph" on pages 3 and 4 to answer Numbers 11–20.

11 Which word from the article meaning "a platform over a section of a ship" is a homograph for the word defined below?

a patio without a roof

Ⓐ deck

Ⓑ dock

Ⓒ sign

Ⓓ trip

12 Read this sentence from the article.

When the boat was being built, Fulton often noticed people making fun of it and joking about it.

What does the idiom *making fun of* mean?

Ⓕ laughing at

Ⓖ being happy about

Ⓗ inventing names for

Ⓘ creating a new game

13 Read this sentence from the article.

People thought it was misnamed the *North River* and should have been called *Fulton's Folly* because it was so foolish.

What does the word *misnamed* mean in this sentence?

Ⓐ named after

Ⓑ named again

Ⓒ without a name

Ⓓ wrongly named

GO ON →

Name: ______________________________ Date: ________

14 Read this sentence from the article.

Fulton reported passing many schooners so quickly that they seemed as if they were anchored.

What does *schooners* mean in the sentence above?

Ⓕ swimmers

Ⓖ water birds

Ⓗ river docks

Ⓘ sailing ships

15 Which sentence from the article supports the idea that people were thankful to be safe after their first ride on a steamboat?

Ⓐ A nervous crowd moved about on a dock on the East River in New York City on August 17, 1807.

Ⓑ Fulton posted a sign seeking passengers for the return trip to New York.

Ⓒ The passengers gladly left the boat for dry land.

Ⓓ It traveled the first 110 miles in just 24 hours.

16 Look at the illustration on page 4. What can you learn about Fulton's steamboat from this illustration?

Ⓕ It could take advantage of both wind and steam power.

Ⓖ It was a dangerous method of transportation.

Ⓗ It had room for only 10 to 20 passengers.

Ⓘ It was designed to be quiet.

GO ON →

Name: ______________________________ Date: __________

17 Why does the author describe the attitudes of the public and Fulton's friends?

Ⓐ to explain the reasons for the design of Fulton's boat

Ⓑ to contrast the feelings of his friends with those of the public

Ⓒ to show the problems Fulton had in getting support for his boat

Ⓓ to describe the problems Fulton had in expanding his steamboat company

18 Read this sentence from the article.

> **One observer thought the boat looked like a sawmill mounted on a flat-bottomed boat and set on fire.**

The author most likely included this statement to explain why Fulton's steamboat

Ⓕ traveled so quickly.

Ⓖ seemed dangerous.

Ⓗ was so interesting.

Ⓘ did not rely solely on wind power.

19 Read these sentences from the article.

> **Land travel was slow and uncomfortable. Shifting winds and tides made sailing the river unpredictable.**

The author included these sentences in order to explain

Ⓐ why Fulton's business grew.

Ⓑ the challenges Fulton faced.

Ⓒ why people preferred steamboat travel.

Ⓓ how hard it was to travel from New York to Albany.

GO ON →

Name: ______________________ Date: __________

20 Both clipper ships and steamboats were new forms of transportation when first used. Compare and contrast steamboats with clipper ships using clear text evidence from the articles.

____

____

____

____

____

____

____

____

____

____

____

____

____

____

____

____

____

____

____

____

____

____

____

GO ON →

Read the passage "Camping Without a Phone" before answering Numbers 21 through 30.

Camping Without a Phone

I couldn't believe it when my parents told me we were going camping during winter vacation. Camping! They are always trying to get me to go outside more. It seems like my mom is always saying, "Brian, turn off the computer!" or "Brian, put down your phone and talk to us!" They don't seem to understand that I'm in the zone when I'm using a keyboard, so of course I don't want to stop.

We drove for an hour to Everglades National Park. As soon as we got there, my cell phone stopped working. The precaution I had taken of fully charging it had done no good. I couldn't get a signal for it. Suddenly, I was facing three days of no contact with the outside world. My little brother, Ben, thought it was funny, and my mom tried to tell me I'd like it. "You'll be able to look around more when you're not staring at a screen," she said.

"You might have to act like a human being," said Ben as he started laughing. Then he ran to the other side of the campground.

We took a hike with a ranger in the afternoon. At first, I couldn't care less, but after a while I started listening. By the end of the hike, I realized there was more action going on in the park than in most video games. It just didn't happen as obviously.

First, the ranger explained that fires can be good for the Everglades. Lightning starts the fires. The pines and some other trees resist fire, and their branches are too high for the fires to reach. Other trees and plants that try to take over from the pines are lower and get burned away. I could almost envision the fires burning around us while we walked, as if they were on a video screen.

GO ON →

Then we stopped to look at what a bobcat had left behind. It was a pile of fur and little bones. They were probably the remains of a rabbit. The ranger said that bobcats hunt nearly every night and sometimes eat animals as large as a deer. We didn't get to see the action, but we saw some of the results.

Then we saw a wood stork wading and moving its beak back and forth. It was over three feet tall. It can't see the small fish it's trying to catch because the water is muddy and full of plants. But its beak is very sensitive. When it touches a fish, its beak snaps closed in 25 milliseconds! That's faster than some computer networks respond when I touch a key.

I was really tired that night. We'd done a lot of walking, and I didn't use enough sunscreen. I looked a little like what the ranger called the "tourist tree." The gumbo limbo tree has reddish bark that peels off, like it got sunburned. Even so, I woke up in the middle of the night, and I was scared at first because of some strange sounds. But then I recognized the barred owl the ranger had described. It sounds like it's calling out "Who cooks for you? Who cooks for you?" That helped me calm down, and I went back to sleep.

The next two days we did a lot more exploring. I started to see that all the land and water and animals were connected. In the Everglades, you couldn't even get rid of the mosquitoes without making a big change for other animals. Small fish eat mosquito eggs; other fish eat the smaller fish; large fish called gars eat those fish; and alligators eat the gars. If you got rid of the mosquitoes, you might lose some of the other animals higher up the food chain too.

After we left, we talked in the car about the Everglades and how different it was from where we lived. Right in the middle of our discussion, I heard a familiar tone from my phone. My friend Jeff was sending me a text. I reached for my phone, then put it back down. "Aren't you going to text back?" asked Ben.

"I will in a little while," I said. Ben looked stunned. My dad and mom looked at each other and just smiled.

GO ON →

Name: ______________________________ Date: ________

Now answer Numbers 21–30. Base your answers on the passage "Camping Without a Phone."

21 Read this sentence from the passage.

> **They don't seem to understand that I'm in the zone when I'm using a keyboard, so of course I don't want to stop.**

What does the idiom *in the zone* mean?

Ⓐ typing

Ⓑ not paying attention

Ⓒ waiting to get started

Ⓓ focusing on what you are doing

22 Read this sentence from the passage.

> **The precaution I had taken of fully charging it had done no good.**

The prefix *pre-* shows that the word *precaution* means the narrator

Ⓕ warned others.

Ⓖ planned ahead.

Ⓗ was not warned.

Ⓘ planned many times.

23 Read this sentence from the passage.

> **I could almost envision the fires burning around us while we walked, as if they were on a video screen.**

What does *envision* mean in the sentence above?

Ⓐ hear

Ⓑ feel

Ⓒ see

Ⓓ smell

GO ON →

Name: ______________________ Date: ________

24 How was Ben's reaction to no cell phone signal while camping different from Brian's?

Ⓕ Ben was hoping Brian could use his cell phone, while Brian was not concerned.

Ⓖ Ben was surprised about the lack of signal, while Brian expected it.

Ⓗ Ben was amused, while Brian was concerned.

Ⓘ Ben was upset, while Brian was happy.

25 Brian is upset because

Ⓐ Ben teases him.

Ⓑ his mom criticizes him.

Ⓒ his cell phone won't work in the Everglades.

Ⓓ the ranger doesn't provide enough information about the park.

26 Why doesn't Brian text his friend back right away?

Ⓕ He wants to keep talking to his parents about the Everglades.

Ⓖ He wants to wait until he gets home to do it.

Ⓗ His parents won't let him have his phone.

Ⓘ He can't get a signal on his phone.

27 What is the main setting of the passage?

Ⓐ Brian's room

Ⓑ the family car

Ⓒ a ranger station

Ⓓ Everglades National Park

GO ON →

Name: ______________________________ Date: ________

28 Read these sentences from the end of the passage.

After we left, we talked in the car about the Everglades and how different it was from where we lived. Right in the middle of our discussion, I heard a familiar tone from my phone. My friend Jeff was sending me a text. I reached for my phone, then put it back down. "Aren't you going to text back?" asked Ben.

"I will in a little while," I said. Ben looked stunned. My dad and mom looked at each other and just smiled.

Explain why Brian's parents smile at each other at the end. Use clear text evidence from the passage to support your answer.

____

____

____

____

____

____

29 How does the author make it clear that Brian's problem is solved?

Ⓐ by listing what he sees

Ⓑ by pointing out that he has no cell phone signal

Ⓒ by showing how he reacts to Ben laughing

Ⓓ by identifying the things that interest him

GO ON →

Name: ______________________________ Date: ________

31 What is the best way to correct sentence 1?

Ⓐ I started playing football on a new team this year. Our coach gave us a notebook with plays in it.

Ⓑ I started playing football on a new team this year: our coach gave us a notebook with plays in it.

Ⓒ I started playing football. On a new team this year, our coach gave us a notebook with plays in it.

Ⓓ I started playing football on a new team this year. our coach gave us a notebook with plays in it.

32 Which sentence has an error in capitalization?

Ⓕ Sentence 2

Ⓖ Sentence 3

Ⓗ Sentence 4

Ⓘ Sentence 5

33 Which of these is a sentence fragment?

Ⓐ Sentence 6

Ⓑ Sentence 7

Ⓒ Sentence 8

Ⓓ Sentence 9

34 Which sentence has a compound predicate?

Ⓕ Sentence 3

Ⓖ Sentence 5

Ⓗ Sentence 8

Ⓘ Sentence 12

GO ON →

Name: ______________________________ Date: ________

35 Which of these is a compound sentence?

Ⓐ Sentence 5

Ⓑ Sentence 6

Ⓒ Sentence 8

Ⓓ Sentence 14

36 What is the best way to write sentence 18?

Ⓕ I told the coach before the next game. And he let me play.

Ⓖ I told the coach before the next game, and he let me play.

Ⓗ I told the coach before the next game, he let me play.

Ⓘ I told the coach before the next game but he let me play.

37 What is the best way to write sentence 13?

Ⓐ I came back down, then my dad had checkers spread out on the table.

Ⓑ I came back down, my dad had checkers spread out on the table.

Ⓒ Because I came back down, my dad had checkers spread out on the table.

Ⓓ When I came back down, my dad had checkers spread out on the table.

GO ON →

Name: ______________________ Date: ________

38 Which sentence includes an interjection?

Ⓕ Sentence 5

Ⓖ Sentence 8

Ⓗ Sentence 11

Ⓘ Sentence 16

39 What is the subject of sentence 17?

Ⓐ suddenly

Ⓑ I

Ⓒ got

Ⓓ it

40 Which is the best way of combining sentences 20 and 21 to make a complex sentence?

Ⓕ Playing checkers made me have a good season.

Ⓖ Although I've had a good season, that day we played checkers.

Ⓗ That day we played checkers because I've had a good season.

Ⓘ Since that day we played checkers, I've had a good season.

STOP

Writing Prompt – Narrative

This unit focuses on new ideas and where they came from. Think about your own life. Have you ever had a new idea?

Write a narrative telling about an idea you have had and tell what inspired your idea.

Use the space below to plan your writing. Write your final copy on a clean sheet of paper.

Answer Key

Name: ____________________

Question	Correct Answer	Content Focus	CCSS	Complexity
1	C	Context Clues: Sentence Clues	L.5.4a	DOK 2
2	F	Greek Roots	L.5.4b	DOK 1
3	B	Homographs	L.5.5c	DOK 1
4	F	Author's Point of View	RI.5.8	DOK 3
5	D	Text Structure: Cause and Effect	RI.5.3	DOK 2
6	I	Text Features: Illustrations	RI.5.7	DOK 1
7	C	Text Structure: Cause and Effect	RI.5.3	DOK 2
8	see below	Author's Point of View	RI.5.8	DOK 3
9	see below	Author's Point of View	RI.5.8	DOK 3
10	see below	Text Structure: Cause and Effect	RI.5.3	DOK 2
11	A	Homographs	L.5.5c	DOK 1
12	F	Idioms	L.5.5b	DOK 2
13	D	Greek and Latin Prefixes	L.5.4b	DOK 1
14	I	Context Clues: Sentence Clues	L.5.4a	DOK 2
15	C	Author's Point of View	RI.5.8	DOK 3
16	F	Text Features: Illustrations	RI.5.7	DOK 2
17	C	Author's Point of View	RI.5.8	DOK 3
18	G	Text Structure: Cause and Effect	RI.5.3	DOK 2
19	A	Text Structure: Cause and Effect	RI.5.3	DOK 2
20	see below	Comparing Across Texts	RI.5.9	DOK 4
21	D	Idioms	L.5.5b	DOK 2
22	G	Greek and Latin Prefixes	L.5.4b	DOK 1

Answer Key

Name: ______________________________

Question	Correct Answer	Content Focus	CCSS	Complexity
23	C	Context Clues: Sentence Clues	L.5.4a	DOK 2
24	H	Character, Setting, Plot: Sequence	RL.3.3	DOK 1
25	C	Character, Setting, Plot: Problem and Solution	RL.4.3	DOK 2
26	F	Character, Setting, Plot: Problem and Solution	RL.4.3	DOK 2
27	D	Character, Setting, Plot: Setting	RL.5.3	DOK 1
28	see below	Character, Setting, Plot: Problem and Solution	RL.5.1	DOK 2
29	D	Character, Setting, Plot: Problem and Solution	RL.4.3	DOK 2
30	see below	Character, Setting, Plot: Problem and Solution	RL.4.3	DOK 2
31	A	Run-on Sentences and Fragments	L.4.1f	DOK 1
32	H	Sentences	L.4.2a	DOK 1
33	A	Run-on Sentences and Fragments	L.4.1f	DOK 1
34	F	Subjects and Predicates	L.5.1	DOK 1
35	D	Compound Sentences and Conjunctions	L.5.1a	DOK 1
36	G	Compound Sentences and Conjunctions	L.5.1a	DOK 1
37	D	Complex Sentences	L.5.2b	DOK 1
38	H	Sentences	L.5.1a	DOK 1
39	B	Subjects and Predicates	L.5.1	DOK 1
40	I	Complex Sentences	L.5.2b	DOK 1
Prompt	see below	Narrative Writing	W.5.3a–e	DOK 3

Comprehension: Multiple-Choice 4, 5, 6, 7, 15, 16, 17, 18, 19, 24, 25, 26, 27, 29	/14	%
Comprehension: Constructed Response 8, 9, 10, 20, 28, 30	/16	%
Vocabulary 1, 2, 3, 11, 12, 13, 14, 21, 22, 23	/10	%
Grammar, Mechanics, Usage 31–40	/10	%
Total Unit Assessment Score	/50	%

 Name: ____________________

8 **2-point item.** The author admires or appreciates clipper ships. Details that support this view include the author describing clipper ships as the most beautiful sailing ships ever built, as seeming to fly across the water, and carrying valuable cargo all around the world.

9 **2-point item.** The author makes the point that it is natural for traders to choose the fastest type of transportation because their goal is to beat their competitors.

10 **2-point item.** The author suggests that the reason clipper ships were developed was to better meet the economic goal for transportation: traders wanted to be able to ship goods—and people—from one place to another in the shortest amount of time. Students should note this same reason as the basis for other changes in transportation, such as steamboats and railroads.

20 **4-point item.** Students should note that both the clipper ship and steamboat triggered major changes in transportation when they were introduced. Clipper ships and steamboats can be compared in the following ways: Both became very popular shortly after they were introduced because they increased the speed of delivery of both cargo and passengers. They were both very important because they changed the ways that freight and passengers were transported. Clipper ships and steamboats can be contrasted in the following ways: Clipper ships were some of the most beautiful sailing vessels ever built, while steamboats were far from beautiful, spewing smoke and sparks and appearing as if they might blow up at any time. Clipper ships were also used mainly for delivering cargo around the world, while steamboats were mainly used for moving cargo and passengers within the United States.

28 **2-point item.** Brian's parents are smiling because, before the camping trip, Brian would have stopped talking to them and responded to the text right away. Brian's parents are probably happy about the camping trip because it helped Brian develop a little more appreciation for nature. It also showed him that getting away from computers and talking with his family about an interesting subject can be enjoyable and important.

30 **4-point item.** At the beginning, Brian is shocked that he has to go camping and does not want to leave his computer or his phone. He is upset that he has to go outside and is not interested in nature or relating to his family. After hiking with a ranger and learning a lot about the Everglades, Brian shows some appreciation for nature and seems to enjoy talking and being with his family.

Writing Prompt

Refer to the scoring criteria in the Teacher Introduction to assess written responses to the prompt.

Read the next two articles. Then answer the questions that follow.

How Green Is Greensburg?

A few years ago, not many people outside of Kansas had ever heard of the little town of Greensburg (population 1,500). Its main claim to fame was a tourist attraction, the World's Largest Hand-Dug Well. But today, the town is known all over the world. Given the town's name, it is fitting that its fame now comes from being "green."

May 4, 2007

Folks in Greensburg didn't think much of it when the weather reports predicted thunderstorms. Even a tornado watch was not unusual. That doesn't mean residents don't take twisters seriously. When alarm sirens told them that a tornado had actually been spotted nearby, they moved quickly into basements and storm shelters.

At 9:45 P.M., the tornado crashed into Greensburg. It measured about 1.7 miles across, nearly as wide as the entire town. Its swirling winds were moving at more than 200 miles per hour. Like a gigantic, out-of-control bulldozer, the tornado zigzagged through Greensburg. When it finally moved on, it had demolished about 95 percent of the town. Homes, businesses, schools, churches, the hospital, even the trees—all destroyed or badly damaged. The electricity was out, and water supplies could not be trusted. Even worse, ten people had been killed.

Timeline for Greensburg Tornado

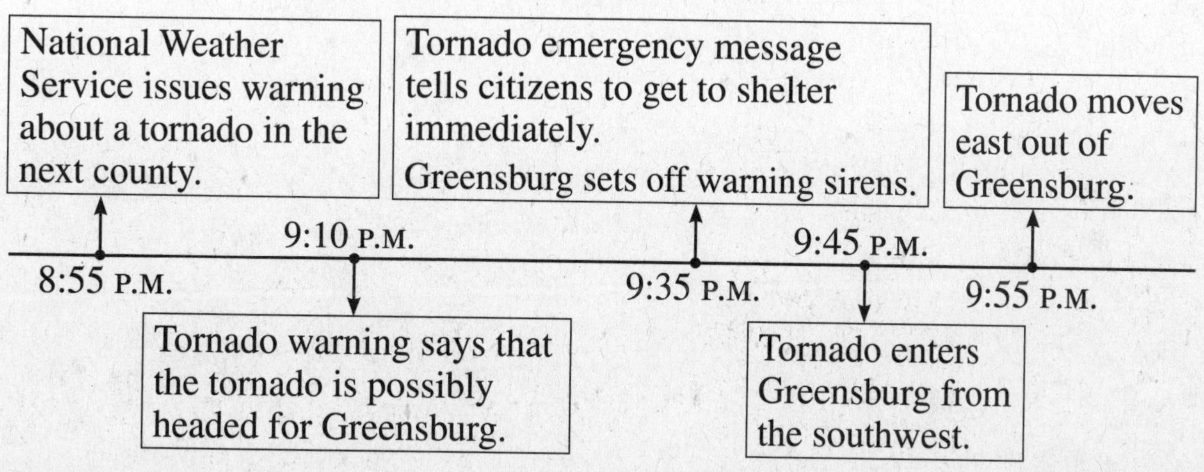

GO ON →

Planning a New Direction

Less than a week after the tornado, the community made the decision that would change Greensburg forever. The people decided that they would rebuild the town green—that is, in ways that were good for the environment. City buildings would use eco-friendly materials and be energy efficient. Citizens would build new homes the same way. Electricity would come from alternative energy sources, such as the wind and sun. Instead of giving up on Greensburg, people got excited about its future.

Building a New Town

Greensburg moved ahead quickly. Of course, the first challenge was just keeping the town going. Government and other sources helped provide basic services and housing. City offices were set up in trailers. So were the hospital and school.

In October 2009, Greensburg started constructing a wind farm with giant windmills. The wind farm would supply energy for the town. The new county hospital that opened in March 2010 was built to strict LEED standards. (LEED stands for a program called Leadership in Energy and Environmental Design. Its purpose is to support green construction.) The town hall, courthouse, and arts center are also LEED buildings. The new school for grades K–12 was finished in August 2010. It has natural daytime lighting and other energy-efficient features. Nearly half the homes in town were rebuilt according to green guidelines. Even the streetlights are designed to use less energy and reduce nighttime light pollution.

GO ON →

One of the most exciting parts of the rebuilding is the Chain of Eco-Homes Project. It was launched in early 2009. The plan was to build 12 homes in different designs that demonstrate state-of-the-art green living. The structures would serve as information centers. People would be able to stay in them and experience what an environmentally-friendly home is like. The first house was completed in 2010, and two more were started. Building the Eco-Homes provided much-needed jobs for workers in the area. The unique houses help support a new type of business in Greensburg: eco-tourism. Visitors began traveling to Greensburg to see these interesting homes and other sights on the Green Tour. They brought with them much-needed money and attention. This helped Greensburg continue its unusual comeback.

Greensburg Today

Today, Greensburg has only about 770 residents. That is half as many as it had when the tornado struck. With their homes and workplaces destroyed, many people had no choice but to move away. Many others, however, stayed or came back. They moved into trailers and have been rebuilding their lives from the ground up. New people have also been arriving. Most residents really like the direction Greensburg has taken. Every day, someone comes up with a new plan to help it live up to its name. Clearly, Greensburg has a bright future ahead of it—a bright *green* future.

GO ON →

Maureen Connolly: Tennis Star!

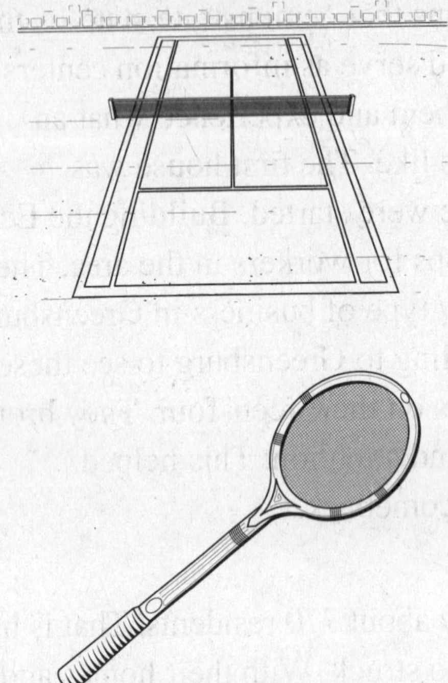

"I think that I could keep on playing even if they set off dynamite in the middle of the court," said Maureen Connolly, a tennis player who won tennis championships in four countries when she was only 19 years old. Many people think that Maureen Connolly was the best female tennis star who ever played.

Maureen Connolly was born in San Diego, California, in 1934. She loved riding horses as a little girl, but her mother could not pay for riding lessons. She asked Maureen to find a less expensive hobby. Maureen decided she wanted to play tennis.

Maureen was very ambitious. That is, she was determined to do whatever it took to achieve her goals. She paid for her first tennis lessons by picking up tennis balls at the tennis courts. She worked hard and won her first tennis tournament just a few months later. After that taste of victory, Maureen had found the sport she loved. She dedicated three hours a day to tennis.

Maureen, who was only 5'4" and 120 pounds, needed a special tennis racket because her hands were so small. But Maureen proved that small players could be powerful too. At age 14 she won 56 tennis

GO ON →

matches in a row! She then became the youngest girl to win the Female Under 18 United States Championship. Fans found Maureen irresistible and loved watching her play. She spent lots of time signing her name on photos when people asked for her autograph. When people started calling her "Little Mo," she went along with it. After all, "Big Mo" was a famous battleship of that time, strong and powerful.

When Maureen was 16 years old, she became the youngest female ever to win the U.S. Open, the biggest tennis tournament in the country. One sports reporter called her a "killer on the courts" because of the way she hit the ball. In 1953, Maureen won the four biggest tennis tournaments in the world. She won the championships in Australia, England, the United States, and France.

Maureen was also the youngest female player ever to win the Wimbledon tournament in England. By the age of 20, she was the number one female tennis player in the world. She was also named the Associated Press Woman Athlete of the Year for three years in a row. Then, in 1954, just a few weeks after winning her third Wimbledon tournament, Maureen was in a terrible accident. She was hit by a truck while horseback riding. One of her legs was badly crushed. Maureen then turned her powers to getting well. She tried to play tennis again, but the damage to her leg was too severe. At the age of 20, "Little Mo" retired from tennis.

Yet real champions go on winning in other ways. Soon, she began writing a sports column for a local newspaper. She also taught tennis to children and teenagers. Maureen and her husband, Norman Brinker, wanted to found a group that would help create tennis programs for young players. To do so, they started the Maureen Connolly Brinker Foundation.

Maureen died from cancer at only 34 years old. But in her short life, she enjoyed much success.

GO ON →

Name: ______________________________ Date: __________

Use "How Green is Greensburg?" on pages 27–29 to answer Numbers 1 through 10.

1. What is the purpose of the headings in this article?

   Ⓐ to point out the most important information

   Ⓑ to convince people to read the article

   Ⓒ to show what each section is about

   Ⓓ to explain what the title means

2. The timeline is important to the article because it shows

   Ⓕ where the alarm sirens were.

   Ⓖ how quickly the tornado struck.

   Ⓗ how much damage the tornado caused.

   Ⓘ who reported the tornado in the next county.

3. What does the timeline tell the reader about the night of May 4, 2007, and what the people of Greensburg experienced? Use details from the article to support your answer.

   ____

   ____

   ____

   ____

   ____

   ____

GO ON →

Name: ______________________________ Date: ________

4 Read these sentences from the article.

When it finally moved on, it had demolished about 95 percent of the town. Homes, businesses, schools, churches, the hospital, even the trees—all destroyed or badly damaged.

What does *demolished* mean in the sentences above?

Ⓕ flooded

Ⓖ involved

Ⓗ missed

Ⓘ wrecked

5 In the section called "Building a New Town," how does the author let the reader know the order of events?

Ⓐ by including the dates of key events

Ⓑ by arranging events in the order they occurred

Ⓒ by using words such as "first," "next," and "last"

Ⓓ by showing how one event resulted from another

6 Which word from the article that means "strong movements of air" is a homograph for the word defined below?

moves along a curving path

Ⓕ centers

Ⓖ parts

Ⓗ twisters

Ⓘ winds

GO ON →

Name: ______________________________ Date: __________

7 Read this sentence from the article.

Its main claim to fame was a tourist attraction, the World's Largest Hand-Dug Well.

The suffix *-ist* helps you understand that *tourist* means

Ⓐ many tours.

Ⓑ without a tour.

Ⓒ able to go on a tour.

Ⓓ someone who goes on a tour.

8 Read this sentence from the article.

Like a gigantic, out-of-control bulldozer, the tornado zigzagged through Greensburg.

Why is the author comparing these two things?

Ⓕ to explain that the winds in a tornado move in a circle

Ⓖ to show that the tornado was very big and did a lot of damage

Ⓗ to point out that every part of Greensburg was affected by the tornado

Ⓘ to show that big heavy machines were needed to clean up after the tornado

GO ON →

Name: ______________________________ Date: ________

9. Why did the author include the detail that the new school in Greensburg was built with natural daytime lighting? Use details from the article to explain.

____

____

____

____

____

____

10. What happened when the residents dealt with the problem of rebuilding Greensburg in the way that they did?

Ⓕ The population doubled.

Ⓖ It became a tourist attraction.

Ⓗ It became safe from future tornadoes.

Ⓘ It began the Chain of Eco-Homes Project.

GO ON →

Name: ______________________________ Date: __________

Use "Maureen Connolly: Tennis Star!" on pages 30 and 31 to answer Numbers 11 through 20.

11 How did the author organize this article?

Ⓐ by describing events in the order they happened

Ⓑ by stating a problem and showing how Maureen solved it

Ⓒ by comparing Maureen's early life to her tennis-playing years

Ⓓ by describing different situations and telling what caused each one

12 Read these sentences from the article.

Maureen was very ambitious. That is, she was determined to do whatever it took to achieve her goals.

What does *ambitious* mean in the sentences above?

Ⓕ greedy

Ⓖ skillful

Ⓗ eager for success

Ⓘ annoying to others

13 What did the sports reporter mean by calling Maureen a "killer on the courts"?

Ⓐ She hit the ball hard enough to tear the net.

Ⓑ She was almost impossible to beat.

Ⓒ She tried to hurt other players.

Ⓓ She was rude to reporters.

GO ON →

Name: ______________________ Date: ________

14 What happened after Maureen won 56 tennis matches in a row but before she won Wimbledon?

Ⓕ She got a special racket.

Ⓖ She wrote a sports column.

Ⓗ She was in a terrible accident.

Ⓘ She won the U.S. Open at age 16.

15 Read this sentence from the article.

Maureen and her husband, Norman Brinker, wanted to found a group that would help create tennis programs for young players.

Which definition of *found* best fits the way it is used in the sentence above?

Ⓐ located

Ⓑ to establish

Ⓒ to pour into a mold

Ⓓ to gain or regain the power of

GO ON →

Name: ______________________________ Date: __________

16 Maureen's family did not have much money when she was a child. How does the author connect this problem to Maureen's tennis playing?

____

____

____

____

____

____

17 Read this sentence from the article.

She spent lots of time signing her name on photos when people asked for her autograph.

Which definition best fits the way *lots* is used in the sentence above?

Ⓐ large amounts or numbers

Ⓑ groups of things that are alike

Ⓒ areas of land for building houses

Ⓓ outdoor areas for filming movies

GO ON →

Name: ______________________________ Date: ________

18 How does the author show how Maureen's small size affected her tennis career? Support your answer with details from the article.

____

____

____

____

____

____

19 During Maureen Connolly's life, which of these events happened last?

Ⓐ She decided her leg was healed enough to play tennis.

Ⓑ She began giving tennis lessons to children.

Ⓒ She won her third Wimbledon tournament.

Ⓓ She retired from playing tennis.

GO ON →

Name: ______________________________ Date: __________

Use "How Green Is Greensburg?" and "Maureen Connolly: Tennis Star!" to answer the question below.

20 With determination and hard work, people can face difficult challenges and overcome them. How do both the people of Greensburg, Kansas, and Maureen Connolly illustrate this idea? Use details from the articles to support your response.

GO ON →

Read the passage "The Prince Who Learned Wisdom" before answering Numbers 21 through 30.

The Prince Who Learned Wisdom

There once lived a prince who would someday become the ruler. "Study hard, my boy," his father would say. "You will need a good education when you become the king."

The prince took these words to heart and studied hard. Then one day, a thought came to him. "My teachers give me a lot of useful *knowledge,* but I wonder if I am gaining the *wisdom* that a ruler needs." He decided the answer was no. To gain wisdom, he needed a new plan.

The prince told his father he wanted to visit a nearby country whose philosophers were said to be very wise. He would ask them to teach him their wisdom. The king thought this was foolish. "Wisdom comes only from a good education," he said. "Your teachers are preparing you very well." Still, he agreed to let his son go and even gave him some gold coins for his journey. Neither suspected that the prince's search would end up taking him in a very different direction.

Early the next morning, the prince set out. To avoid attracting attention, he dressed in ordinary clothes and carried his belongings on his back like anyone else. As he strode along, he whistled a cheerful tune, happy to be out on his own.

By afternoon, he was hungry and sat down in a field to eat his lunch. The warm sun stroking his cheek and the soft breeze whispering in his ears made him drowsy.

The prince was awakened suddenly by the crackling of dry leaves. A thief was running away with his pack! He was too far away to catch, so the prince had to go on without it. (Luckily, the gold coins were hidden inside his coat.) He continued on, pondering what had occurred. As he was thinking deeply, he came to a realization. "Anything can happen when you sleep

GO ON →

outside. When I become the ruler, I must make sure that everyone has a safe place to sleep." Then he laughed. "That fellow actually gave me a bit of wisdom!"

As evening approached, it began to rain. With a long way still to go and his feet soggy, the prince stopped at an inn. Aching with hunger, he welcomed the scents of fresh bread and a stew that met him at the door. After a delicious meal, he went up to his room, blew out the candle, and got into bed—but not for long. CREEEEEAK! A young woman crept into the dark room and took his boots. As she tried to creep out again, the prince leaped up, blocked her way, and yelled for the innkeeper. When the man arrived, the outraged prince informed him the woman had been stealing his boots.

"No, she wasn't," said the innkeeper. "She was taking them downstairs to the fire so they would dry before morning. I'm sorry if my daughter disturbed you."

The prince felt embarrassed and gave the daughter a gold coin as an apology. Back in bed, he thought about what had happened. "When I am king, I must be sure to get all the facts before I make a judgment," he concluded. Then, laughing, "I never expected to acquire wisdom in a village inn!"

The next day, instead of continuing on, the prince went back the way he had come. He did not stop until he was inside the palace.

"Back already?" exclaimed his father. "You can't possibly have made it even to the border. Why did you give up your plan?"

"Father," answered the prince, "in just two days, I gained enough wisdom to know it was not such a good plan. I now realize there is no need to seek wisdom in far-off places. Wisdom can be found anywhere if you pay attention and try to learn from your experiences." This reply greatly pleased the king, who agreed with his son.

From that day on, the prince made a point of leaving the palace at least twice a week to watch and listen to what was happening among the people. When the time came for him to be king, he was a very wise ruler indeed.

GO ON →

Name: ______________________________ Date: ________

Now answer Numbers 21 through 30. Base your answers on "The Prince Who Learned Wisdom."

21 Which sentence best supports the theme of the passage?

Ⓐ There once lived a prince who would someday become the ruler.

Ⓑ "When I am king, I must be sure to get all the facts before I make a judgment."

Ⓒ The next day, instead of continuing on, the prince went back the way he had come.

Ⓓ "Wisdom can be found anywhere if you pay attention and try to learn from your experiences."

22 What is the purpose of the illustration?

Ⓕ to show how the prince's pack was stolen

Ⓖ to explain why the thief wanted the prince's pack

Ⓗ to describe how the prince felt about being robbed

Ⓘ to indicate where the prince's gold coins were hidden

23 What did the prince think was different about the nearby country?

Ⓐ There were more inns.

Ⓑ People there were thieves.

Ⓒ Wise philosophers lived there.

Ⓓ The people often went hungry.

24 Read these sentences from the passage.

> **He continued on, pondering what had occurred. As he was thinking deeply, he came to a realization.**

What words tell you what *pondering* means?

Ⓕ continued on

Ⓖ thinking deeply

Ⓗ a realization

Ⓘ had occurred

GO ON →

Name: ______________________________ Date: ________

25 Read this sentence from the passage.

The prince was awakened suddenly by the crackling of dry leaves.

The author's use of sensory language appeals most to the sense of

Ⓐ hearing.

Ⓑ sight.

Ⓒ smell.

Ⓓ touch/feeling.

26 How are the thief and the innkeeper's daughter alike?

Ⓕ Both try to steal from the prince.

Ⓖ Both end up with some of the prince's gold.

Ⓗ Both recognize the prince in spite of his disguise.

Ⓘ Both teach the prince a lesson without knowing it.

27 Read these sentences from the passage.

By afternoon, he was hungry and sat down in a field to eat his lunch. The warm sun stroking his cheek and the soft breeze whispering in his ears made him drowsy.

What does "warm sun stroking his cheek and the soft breeze whispering in his ears" mean?

Ⓐ Someone touched the prince's head while he was sleeping.

Ⓑ The sun and breeze were especially strong that afternoon.

Ⓒ The sun and breeze were both like a gentle person.

Ⓓ The prince was not used to sleeping outside.

GO ON →

Name: ______________________ Date: ________

28 How is the setting connected to the main problem in this passage?

Ⓕ The prince is comfortable inside the palace but frightened everywhere else.

Ⓖ The only time the prince learns anything is when he falls asleep.

Ⓗ The prince thinks he must travel to a new place to learn wisdom.

Ⓘ The lessons the prince learns make him want to leave home.

29 What do the prince and his father agree about?

Ⓐ Wisdom comes only from a good education.

Ⓑ The prince has succeeded in meeting his goal.

Ⓒ Seeking wisdom from philosophers is a good idea.

Ⓓ The prince's teachers are preparing him fully to be king.

GO ON →

Name: ______________________________ Date: __________

30 Read this sentence from the passage.

Neither suspected that the prince's search would end up taking him in a very different direction.

Why did the author include this sentence near the beginning of the passage? Use details from the passage to explain.

____

____

____

____

____

____

____

____

____

____

____

____

____

____

____

____

____

____

____

____

____

GO ON →

Read the article below. Choose the word or words that correctly complete questions 31–35.

Believe it or not, doctors in the past did not wash their hands before treating patients. They did not know that diseases were spread by germs. They did not even know that germs existed.

In the mid-1800s, two doctors made important __(31)__ about preventing the spread of disease. Ignaz Semmelweis (1818–1865) of Hungary noticed that many new mothers and children were dying from infections. He showed that a lot more survived when __(32)__ and doctors cleaned their hands thoroughly. People made fun of his ideas, but Dr. Semmelweis was right.

Joseph Lister (1827–1912) was a surgeon from __(33)__. In 1865, he decided that germs caused infections. At first he thought germs only spread through the air. Then he realized that a __(34)__ hands and instruments also spread germs. After that, Lister made sure that everything in the operating room was kept very clean, including the patient.

The work of these two men has saved many __(35)__ over the years. Today, doctors and hospitals know how important it is to keep as many germs as possible away from their patients.

GO ON →

Name: ______________________ Date: ________

31 Which answer should go in blank (31)?

Ⓐ discoveries

Ⓑ discovereys

Ⓒ discoverys

32 Which answer should go in blank (32)?

Ⓕ nurse

Ⓖ nurses

Ⓗ nursies

33 Which answer should go in blank (33)?

Ⓐ Great Britain

Ⓑ Great britain

Ⓒ great Britain

34 Which answer should go in blank (34)?

Ⓕ doctors's

Ⓖ doctor's

Ⓗ doctors'

35 Which answer should go in blank (35)?

Ⓐ lifes

Ⓑ livs

Ⓒ lives

GO ON →

The passage below is a first draft that Cheryl wrote. The passage contains mistakes. Read the passage to answer questions 36 through 40.

Why Chipmunks Have Striped Coats

(1) Many years ago, chipmunks did not have stripes on their backs as they do now. (2) They were a plain rusty brown all over. (3) This color made it much easier for their enemies to see them. (4) It was very dangerous being a chipmunk in those days.

(5) One morning, a cat caught a chipmunk and carried it into the kitchen. (6) When the cat's owners yelled, the startled cat dropped its prey. (7) Quickly, the chipmunk scooted away and hid behind the woodstove. (8) The peoples were cooking, and the stove was warm. (9) It burned the chipmunk's fur just a little bit. (10) By the time the chipmunk escaped, it had black, gray, and white stripes all down its back.

(11) The chipmunk found that its new colors gave it protection. (12) The stripes looked like bands of shadow and sunlight, making it much easier to hide from predators. (13) Other chipmunks decided they wanted striped coats too. (14) Soon they were finding ways to sneak into the house and visit the woodstove. (15) That's why today chipmunkses' coats all have stripes.

GO ON →

Name: ______________________ Date: ________

36 What is the prepositional phrase in sentence 1?

Ⓕ Many years ago
Ⓗ on their backs
Ⓖ did not have stripes
Ⓘ as they do now

37 What is the purpose of the prepositional phrase in sentence 7?

Ⓐ to show how the chipmunk ran
Ⓑ to tell where the chipmunk hid
Ⓒ to tell where the stove was
Ⓓ to describe the stove

38 How can sentence 8 best be written?

Ⓕ The peoples' were cooking, and the stove was warm.
Ⓖ The people's was cooking, and the stove was warm.
Ⓗ The people were cooking, and the stove was warm.
Ⓘ The people was cooking, and the stove was warm.

39 Which sentence contains an abstract noun?

Ⓐ Sentence 8
Ⓑ Sentence 10
Ⓒ Sentence 11
Ⓓ Sentence 13

40 How can sentence 15 best be written?

Ⓕ That's why today chipmunks's coats all have stripes.
Ⓖ That's why today chipmunks' coats all have stripes.
Ⓗ That's why today chipmunk's coats all have stripes.
Ⓘ That's why today chipmunks coats all have stripes.

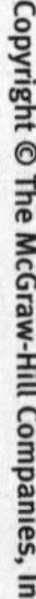

STOP

Writing Prompt – Informative

Suppose that your class is putting together a guidebook for new students to help them understand how things work at your school. Your assignment is to write the section about lunchtime.

Write an informative essay about lunch services at your school. Include any information you think new students would want or need to know, such as where the cafeteria is and what to expect when they get there.

Use the space below to plan your writing. Write your final copy on a clean sheet of paper.

Answer Key

Name: ______________________________

Question	Correct Answer	Content Focus	CCSS	Complexity
1	C	Text Features: Headings	RI.4.7	DOK 2
2	G	Text Features: Timelines	RI.4.7	DOK 2
3	See below	Text Features: Timelines	RI.4.7	DOK 2
4	I	Context Clues: Definitions and Restatements	L.5.4a	DOK 2
5	A	Text Structure: Sequence	RI.5.3	DOK 2
6	I	Homographs	L.5.5c	DOK 1
7	D	Greek and Latin Suffixes	L.5.4b	DOK 1
8	G	Simile	L.5.5a	DOK 2
9	See below	Text Structure: Problem and Solution	RI.5.3	DOK 2
10	G	Problem and Solution	RI.5.3	DOK 2
11	A	Text Structure: Sequence	RI.5.3	DOK 2
12	H	Context Clues: Definitions and Restatements	L.5.4a	DOK 2
13	B	Metaphor	L.5.5a	DOK 2
14	I	Sequence	RI.5.3	DOK 1
15	B	Homographs	L.5.5c	DOK 1
16	See below	Text Structure: Problem and Solution	RI.5.3	DOK 2
17	A	Homographs	L.5.5c	DOK 1
18	See below	Text Structure: Problem and Solution	RI.5.3	DOK 2
19	B	Sequence	RI.5.3	DOK 1
20	See below	Text Structure: Problem and Solution	RI.5.3	DOK 4
21	D	Theme	RL.5.2	DOK 3
22	F	Text Features: Use Illustrations and Photographs	RL.4.7	DOK 2

Answer Key

Name: ____________________

Question	Correct Answer	Content Focus	CCSS	Complexity
23	C	Character, Setting, Plot: Compare and Contrast	RL.5.1	DOK 2
24	G	Context Clues: Definitions and Restatements	L.5.4a	DOK 2
25	A	Literary Elements: Imagery	RL.5.1	DOK 2
26	I	Character, Setting, Plot: Compare and Contrast	RL.5.3	DOK 2
27	C	Personification	L.5.5a	DOK 2
28	H	Character, Setting, Plot: Compare and Contrast	RL.5.3	DOK 2
29	B	Character, Setting, Plot: Compare and Contrast	RL.5.3	DOK 3
30	See below	Literary Elements: Foreshadowing	RL.5.1	DOK 3
31	A	Singular and Plural Nouns	L.5.2	DOK 1
32	G	Singular and Plural Nouns	L.5.2	DOK 1
33	A	Nouns	L.5.2	DOK 1
34	G	Possessive Nouns	L.5.2	DOK 1
35	C	Plural Nouns	L.5.2	DOK 1
36	H	Nouns in Prepositional Phrases	L.5.1a	DOK 1
37	B	Nouns in Prepositional Phrases	L.5.1a	DOK 1
38	H	Plural Nouns	L.5.2	DOK 1
39	C	Nouns	L.5.1	DOK 1
40	G	Possessive Nouns	L.5.2	DOK 1
Prompt	See below	Informative Writing	W.5.2a–e	DOK 3

Comprehension: Multiple-Choice 1, 2, 5, 10, 11, 14, 19, 21, 22, 23, 25, 26, 28, 29	/14	%
Comprehension: Constructed Response 3, 9, 16, 18, 20, 30	/16	%
Vocabulary 4, 6, 7, 8, 12, 13, 15, 17, 24, 27	/10	%
Grammar, Mechanics, Usage 31–40	/10	%
Total Unit Assessment Score	/50	%

3 **2-point item.** The timeline shows that the people of Greensburg received warnings of a possible tornado at 9:10 P.M. At 9:35, they realized that the tornado was approaching. They had only 10 minutes to take shelter, and the tornado destroyed almost everything in town in about 10 minutes.

9 **2-point item.** The sentence is in a paragraph about green buildings that have been built in Greensburg so far. The school is one of several examples that the author includes to show how committed Greensburg is to its green plan. Its natural lighting and energy-efficient features make it an Earth-friendly building.

16 **2-point item.** The author says that Maureen started playing tennis because she could not afford to take horseback riding lessons. She wanted a hobby, so she played tennis instead. To earn money for her tennis lessons, she picked up tennis balls for other players.

18 **2-point item.** The author includes details showing that Maureen made adjustments for her small size and did not let it get in her way. She got a special racket for her small hands. She played very hard. She had a nickname suggesting small size but also power and strength.

20 **4-point item.** When the tornado destroyed Greensburg, people could have just given up and moved someplace else, or they could have just rebuilt everything the same way it was before. Instead, they decided to make something new and exciting. By working together, they rebuilt Greensburg as a "green" town.

Maureen Connolly was terribly injured when hit by a truck. She tried to play tennis again but could not. She had been the best in the world, so people would have understood if she just gave up. She did not, though. Instead, she shared her tennis skills with others by teaching and writing. She also started an organization to help young tennis players. She faced her challenge and overcame it.

30 **4-point item.** The author included this sentence to grab the reader's interest by giving a hint about something that will happen later. It tells the reader that the story may turn out differently from how it looks now, so keep reading. The prince starts out planning to visit some philosophers. He never gets there but instead turns around after one night when he realizes that he can learn wisdom from everyday situations and ordinary people. This is the "different direction" that the sentence talks about. He accomplishes his goal but not the way he expected.

Writing Prompt

Refer to the scoring criteria in the Teacher Introduction to assess written responses to the prompt.

Read the next two articles. Then answer the questions that follow.

Finding Gold, Finding Florida

In 1493, Christopher Columbus sailed again to the Americas. He and others surmised that he had found islands near Asia on his first trip. For that reason, the crew on this trip numbered 1,500 men on 17 ships. One of the crewmen was Juan Ponce de León. He stayed in the New World after Columbus returned to Spain.

Ponce de León was a skilled soldier. He helped defend the Spanish settlers on the island of Hispaniola from native attacks. As a reward, he was named a governor of the island.

The natives told stories and legends of the area. One told of an island to the east called Borinquen where there was gold. Ponce de León was sent to explore the island. When the Spanish landed, they had to fight the native Taino people. The Spanish won, partly because they used dogs in battle. The natives had never seen dogs before, and these fearsome animals were more frightening than the soldiers.

Ponce de León built the first European settlement on Borinquen in 1508. The Spanish soon found gold and forced the native people to mine it. The island was renamed Puerto Rico, meaning "rich port." Ponce de León quickly became rich.

The king then allowed Ponce de León to claim areas north of Hispaniola for Spain. But the king did not provide any ships. Ponce de León used his wealth to buy ships and supplies. Natives told of an island called Bimini to the north where he could find more gold.

They may have also told about a spring that could make people young again. Today, Ponce de León is best known for searching for this "fountain of youth." But there is no proof that Ponce de León ever heard the legend, since none of his writings survived. He did believe he was close to Asia. He may have known that Alexander the Great of Macedonia had unsuccessfully searched for a fountain of youth in Asia 1,800 years before. If Ponce de León did search for a similar source of youth, his search was as fruitless as Alexander the Great's.

GO ON →

The ships sailed north in 1513. They made a few stops at islands in the Bahamas. When they saw the coast of Florida, they thought it was an island, too. They probably landed first near modern-day St. Augustine. They claimed the land for Spain. Ponce de León named it La Florida, meaning "the place of flowers." He must have noted the rainbow colors and sweet smells of the flowers.

His ships sailed down the east coast of Florida. They stopped on islands they named the Dry Tortugas. They found little fresh water but many large sea turtles. Sea turtles are called *tortugas* in Spanish. Later, they tried to land on the west coast of Florida. They soon found that the Calusa people living there were not friendly. So they left Florida and returned to Puerto Rico.

In 1521, Ponce de León returned to the west coast of Florida. He had two ships and 200 men. They wanted to build a settlement. But the Calusa people attacked them again. Ponce de León was wounded in the leg with an arrow. Some thought it was poisoned. The Spanish returned to Puerto Rico, where Ponce de León died soon afterward.

Other explorers realized before long that Florida was not an island and was not in Asia. Spain controlled many areas in the Caribbean and Latin America for more than 300 years. Ponce de León did not find a fountain of youth. But his voyages spurred others to search for gold and other riches in the New World.

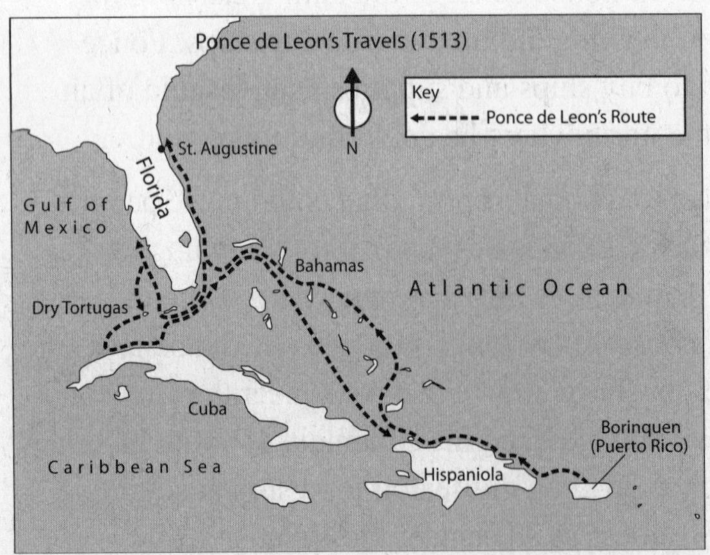

GO ON →

Pioneering in Florida

Ben Hill Doster moved his family from Atlanta, Georgia, to Jupiter, Florida, in 1894 to help his sister. Her husband had died, but she hoped to own 160 acres of land there as a homestead. She just needed to live on it for one more year.

Soon after they arrived, Ben Doster took his family on a boat ride up the Loxahatchee River. Suddenly, the air turned cold. Feeling agitated, Doster rowed hurriedly back to the tiny cabin. The family huddled inside near a roaring fire. That night they heard sounds like gunshots. They turned out to be the trunks of orange trees exploding when they froze. The next morning, they awoke to find their 16-acre pineapple patch frozen. Their garden vegetables were dead, too.

Many new settlers left soon after the Big Freeze of 1894, but the Doster family stayed. They replanted their pineapples and their garden. They also opened up a general store. Slowly, Doster's wife and two daughters learned to love the land of southern Florida and respect its dangers.

In their first year, they began to recognize the sounds of the swamp at night. They thought of it as a nightly serenade. Different types of frogs had distinctive calls. The tiniest frogs chirped "tea table, tea table." The bullfrogs boomed "rung, rung, rung." Owls hooted and birds called to their mates. Sometimes, alligators bellowed.

But one night they awoke to hear the painful scream of a woman. She sounded like she was nearby, so Mrs. Doster prepared to go outside to look for her. But Ben Doster stopped her at the door. He explained that when panthers screamed in the night, they sounded exactly like a woman in pain. No one should go outside to help. Panthers were dangerous.

The family gradually came to know their neighbors and the people who came to the Dosters' store. Some were homesteaders like themselves. These included the local doctor and a man who had gone to Princeton University in New Jersey. Another neighbor claimed to be a member of an English royal family.

GO ON →

Other people had been in the area for generations. These included a few African Americans. They were descendants of runaway slaves who had fled to Florida in the early 1800s. Other families were descendants of early white settlers. They lived in the swamps and continued to make their living by hunting, trapping, and fishing. Sometimes families of Seminole Indians would suddenly appear, using trails through the swamps that no one else could follow. They would camp near a trail to sell deer and alligator hides, bird feathers, and dried venison from deer hunting. They were members of the few families who survived the Seminole Wars of the 1800s and the removal of most of the Seminoles to reservations in the West.

One of Doster's daughters, Dora, later wrote about her memories of the time. She wrote lovingly of mangrove and cypress trees hung with Spanish moss. She saw white herons standing like statues waiting to pluck a fish from the shallow water. Yellow and orange butterflies danced down a path in front of her. She thought the ocean before a hurricane looked like a vicious monster, curling its jaws and showing its teeth. She learned to watch for the poisonous snakes that lived along the paths.

Dora's mother was a strong and brave woman. She stood up to panthers, alligators, and hurricanes. But for her, there was more than danger, beauty, and excitement. Dora's father worked long hours at the store. Dora thought her mother must have gotten very homesick and lonely at the cabin. She saw her mother watch the trains pass to the east and listen to their mournful wails. Dora believed she often wanted to be on one of those trains, headed back home. She had grown up in Atlanta and had not planned to become a pioneer.

GO ON →

Name: ______________________________ Date: ________

Use "Finding Gold, Finding Florida" on pages 55 and 56 to answer Numbers 1 through 10.

1 Read these sentences from the article.

He and others surmised that he had found islands near Asia on his first trip. For that reason, the crew on this trip numbered 1,500 men on 17 ships.

What does *surmised* mean in the sentence above?

Ⓐ battled

Ⓑ doubted

Ⓒ figured

Ⓓ wished

2 Read this sentence from the article.

The natives had never seen dogs before, and these fearsome animals were more frightening than the soldiers.

What does *fearsome* mean in the sentence above?

Ⓕ bold

Ⓖ friendly

Ⓗ terrifying

Ⓘ unusual

3 Read this sentence from the article.

But there is no proof that Ponce de León ever heard the legend, since none of his writings survived.

The root of *survived* is *viv*, meaning "life." This shows that Ponce de León's writing

Ⓐ do not exist.

Ⓑ are not popular.

Ⓒ have been found.

Ⓓ are difficult to read.

GO ON →

Name: ______________________________ Date: ________

4 Read these sentences from the article.

He may have known that Alexander the Great of Macedonia had unsuccessfully searched for a fountain of youth in Asia 1,800 years before. If Ponce de León did search for a similar source of youth, his search was as fruitless as Alexander the Great's.

Fruitless means the search was

Ⓕ difficult.

Ⓖ fun.

Ⓗ a failure.

Ⓘ a success.

5 What sentence from the text is evidence of sensory language?

Ⓐ The Spanish soon found gold and forced the native people to mine it.

Ⓑ He must have noted the rainbow colors and sweet smells of the flowers.

Ⓒ Spain controlled many areas in the Caribbean and Latin America for more than 300 years.

Ⓓ Natives told of an island called Bimini to the north where he could find more gold.

6 What evidence from the text does the author use to question whether Ponce de León actually searched for the "fountain of youth"?

Ⓕ He was encouraged to claim new lands for Spain.

Ⓖ He wanted to build a settlement on the west coast of Florida.

Ⓗ He was interested in gold and islands that might be a source of it.

Ⓘ None of his writings survived to show that he had heard the legend.

GO ON →

Name: ______________________________ Date: ________

7 Why did Ponce de León's group leave the west coast of Florida in 1513?

Ⓐ There was little fresh water.

Ⓑ They wanted to find the island of Bimini.

Ⓒ They found no gold in the "place of flowers."

Ⓓ They found that the people living there were not friendly.

8 What is the purpose of the map that goes with this article?

____

____

____

____

____

____

9 One of the details the author includes to support the idea that Ponce de León inspired later explorers is that he

Ⓐ fought the Taino people.

Ⓑ claimed Florida for Spain.

Ⓒ was wounded in the leg by an arrow.

Ⓓ may have searched for a "fountain of youth."

GO ON →

Name: ______________________________ Date: ________

10 How did Ponce de León interact with natives in the New World, and how successful were his interactions? Use clear text evidence from the article to support your answer.

____

____

____

____

____

____

GO ON →

Name: ______________________________ Date: __________

Use "Pioneering in Florida" on pages 57 and 58 to answer Numbers 11 through 20.

11 Read these sentences from the article.

In their first year, they began to recognize the sounds of the swamp at night. They thought of it as a nightly serenade.

What does *serenade* mean in the sentence above?

Ⓐ movie
Ⓑ opportunity
Ⓒ problem
Ⓓ song

12 Read this sentence from the article.

Feeling agitated, Doster rowed hurriedly back to the tiny cabin.

The origin of the word *agitated* is the Latin word *agitare*, meaning "to put in constant motion, drive onward." What does *agitated* mean in the sentence above?

Ⓕ curious
Ⓖ disturbed
Ⓗ exhausted
Ⓘ relaxed

13 Read these sentences from the article.

Different types of frogs had distinctive calls. The tiniest frogs chirped "tea table, tea table." The bullfrogs boomed "rung, rung, rung."

What does *distinctive* mean in the sentence above?

Ⓐ very loud
Ⓑ frightening
Ⓒ different from others
Ⓓ named after familiar objects

GO ON →

Name: ______________________________ Date: ________

14 What evidence in the text supports the idea that Dora Doster enjoyed pioneering in Florida?

Ⓕ Dora's mother got very homesick.

Ⓖ Dora was afraid of the ocean before a hurricane.

Ⓗ Dora wrote lovingly of the landscape and animals.

Ⓘ The Doster family chose to stay in Florida after the Big Freeze.

15 Why did the Doster family move to Florida?

Ⓐ Ben Doster's wife was unhappy in Atlanta.

Ⓑ Ben Doster wanted to help his sister get her homestead.

Ⓒ The Doster family wanted to plant and grow pineapples.

Ⓓ The Dosters did not want their children to grow up in a city.

16 The author says that butterflies "danced down a path" in order to suggest that they were

Ⓕ moving in pairs.

Ⓖ lively and graceful.

Ⓗ moving in time to music.

Ⓘ colorful, like ball gowns.

17 Based on text evidence, what is the author's attitude about the Dosters? Use information from the article that supports the author's point of view.

____

____

____

____

____

____

GO ON →

Name: ______________________________ Date: ________

18 What text evidence supports the author's point that the Dosters had to be very careful?

Ⓕ He explained that when panthers screamed in the night, they sounded exactly like a woman in pain.

Ⓖ Owls hooted and birds called to their mates.

Ⓗ Many new settlers left soon after the Big Freeze of 1894, but the Doster family stayed.

Ⓘ Dora thought her mother must have gotten very homesick and lonely at the cabin.

19 What did Dora Doster sometimes view as dangerous?

Ⓐ bullfrogs

Ⓑ white herons

Ⓒ Spanish moss

Ⓓ the ocean

GO ON →

Name: ______________________ Date: __________

Use "Finding Gold, Finding Florida" and "Pioneering in Florida" to answer the question below.

20 Both Ponce de León and the Doster family traveled to new areas and made discoveries. Compare and contrast the reasons why Ponce de León and the Doster family went to Florida and what they found there. Support your answer with clear text evidence from both articles.

GO ON →

Read the passage "A Town's History" before answering Numbers 21 through 30.

A Town's History

Lily glanced up at the clock. The minute hand was crawling slowly. There was still more than an hour until lunchtime. Lily could hear her stomach complaining. She slumped down in her seat and started to fiddle with the pencils on her desk.

"Is the speaker going to be here soon, Mr. Gardiner?" Kevin asked the teacher. On Monday, the teacher had told the class that they were going to have a mystery speaker on Friday. All week, everyone had been trying to guess who it was.

"What about the president?" Steven asked. Everyone laughed at the idea of the president of the United States coming to talk to the fifth-grade glass in their small town in Oregon.

"Okay, class, settle down," said Mr. Gardiner. "I can tell you that our speaker will be Ms. Traynor. She works at the museum, and she is going to talk to us about our town's history."

"History is so boring," Lily thought to herself. "I can't imagine anything interesting ever happened here."

Just then, there was a knock at the door, and the principal came in with a woman. Mr. Gardiner introduced her to the class.

"Your teacher has told me that you are studying the Oregon Trail," Ms. Traynor said. "Does anyone know how this town is part of the trail's history?"

GO ON →

"It's where the Oregon Trail ended," Bethany answered.

"That's right. Today, I'm going to tell you about some of the first settlers in our town." Ms. Traynor began to display some black and white photographs. Some were faded at the corners. Many showed people posing stiffly for the camera. There were some of children.

Lily liked looking at the photographs. It was fun seeing what people wore back then. One photograph showed a woman in a long dress with long sleeves. "She must have sweltered in that outfit, like I do when I wear a sweatshirt on a warm day," she thought.

"One of the ways we study history is to read the letters people wrote to friends and family and the journals the people kept for themselves," Ms. Traynor explained.

"Where do you get the journals and letters?" was Steven's query.

"People donate them to the museum so we don't have to buy them. Many of the people who live here are descendants of the first settlers. Sometimes people have saved letters and journals from their great-grandparents. Other people find letters and journals when they are cleaning out houses. I am going to share some of the journals and letters with you today."

In one letter, a woman told her sister back east about a trip on the Oregon Trail. She described long, hot, dusty days on the trail. She wrote about crossing a river on a small, wooden raft.

When Ms. Traynor passed around a journal that had been discovered in someone's attic, Lily couldn't wait to look at it. It was written by a girl who was about Lily's age. She turned the pages of the small book carefully. She saw that the girl wrote about her new town and her new school.

Then suddenly, Ms. Traynor said, "I know you all have to go to lunch, so I will stop now."

Lily looked up at the clock and saw that it was 12:30. The hour had flown by. Then Lily thought about her grandmother's attic. She knew her grandmother kept family letters and journals. What kinds of stories could Lily find in those journals? She couldn't wait to find out.

GO ON →

Name: ______________________________ Date: __________

Now answer Numbers 21 through 30. Base your answers on "A Town's History."

21 Read this sentence from the passage.

> **"Where do you get the journals and letters?" was Steven's query.**

The word *query* comes from the Latin word *quaere*, meaning "ask." What does *query* mean in the sentence above?

Ⓐ interruption

Ⓑ question

Ⓒ reaction

Ⓓ remark

22 Read this sentence from the passage.

> **"She must have sweltered in that outfit, like I do when I wear a sweatshirt on a warm day," she thought.**

What does *sweltered* mean in the sentence above?

Ⓕ looked nice

Ⓖ felt overly hot

Ⓗ felt well-dressed

Ⓘ been proud of herself

23 Read these sentences from the passage.

> **"People donate them to the museum so we don't have to buy them."**

What does *donate* mean in the sentence above?

Ⓐ charge

Ⓑ copy

Ⓒ give

Ⓓ show

GO ON →

Name: ______________________ Date: ________

24 Read this sentence from the passage.

Lily could hear her stomach complaining.

The author uses *complaining* to describe what Lily hears her stomach doing in order to suggest that

Ⓕ the noise is loud.

Ⓖ Lily is feeling hungry.

Ⓗ Lily herself is unhappy.

Ⓘ Lily is rarely satisfied with anything.

25 What is the theme of this passage?

Ⓐ History can be interesting.

Ⓑ Schools need more guest speakers.

Ⓒ Traveling on the Oregon Trail was hard.

Ⓓ People should keep journals about what they do.

26 Which sentences best support the theme of the story?

Ⓕ "Many of the people who live here are descendants of the first settlers. Sometimes people have saved letters and journals from their great-grandparents."

Ⓖ Ms. Traynor began to display some black and white photographs. Some were faded at the corners.

Ⓗ The minute hand was crawling slowly. There was still more than an hour until lunchtime.

Ⓘ What kinds of stories could Lily find in those journals? She couldn't wait to find out.

GO ON →

Name: ______________________ Date: ________

27 The narrator of this passage helps us understand Lily's feelings mainly by

Ⓐ telling what Lily says.

Ⓑ telling Lily's thoughts.

Ⓒ describing what Lily does.

Ⓓ showing how others react to Lily.

28 Read these sentences from the passage.

"History is so boring," Lily thought to herself. "I can't imagine anything interesting ever happened here."

How are Lily's feelings different by the end of the passage? Use details from the passage to explain how and why her feelings changed.

____

____

____

____

____

____

29 What sentence is an example of sensory language?

Ⓐ Sometimes people have saved letters and journals from their great-grandparents.

Ⓑ All week, everyone had been trying to guess who it was.

Ⓒ She saw that the girl wrote about her new town and her new school.

Ⓓ She described long, hot, dusty days on the trail.

GO ON →

Name: ______________________________ Date: __________

31 How can sentence 1 best be written?

Ⓐ One of our most important drugs, penicillin come from mold.

Ⓑ One of our most important drugs, mold, comes from penicillin.

Ⓒ Penicillin, one of our most important drugs, comes from mold.

Ⓓ Penicillin, one of our most important drugs, coming from mold.

32 Which sentence has an action verb?

Ⓕ Sentence 2

Ⓖ Sentence 4

Ⓗ Sentence 17

Ⓘ Sentence 19

33 Which sentence incorrectly shifts tense from past to present?

Ⓐ Sentence 2

Ⓑ Sentence 3

Ⓒ Sentence 4

Ⓓ Sentence 5

34 How can sentence 6 best be written?

Ⓕ He see that the mucus killed the bacteria growing in the dish.

Ⓖ He saw that the mucus killed the bacteria growing in the dish.

Ⓗ He seed that the mucus killed the bacteria growing in the dish.

Ⓘ He was seeing that the mucus killed the bacteria growing in the dish.

GO ON →

Name: ______________________ Date: ________

35 How can sentence 12 best be written?

Ⓐ Later, he noticed that mold was grown on one of the dishes.

Ⓑ Later, he noticed that mold had grown on one of the dishes.

Ⓒ Later, he noticed that mold growed on one of the dishes.

Ⓓ Later, he noticed that mold grow on one of the dishes.

36 Which sentence uses the past progressive tense?

Ⓕ Sentence 2

Ⓖ Sentence 3

Ⓗ Sentence 5

Ⓘ Sentence 7

37 Which sentence indicates that Fleming's work was on-going?

Ⓐ Sentence 2

Ⓑ Sentence 8

Ⓒ Sentence 17

Ⓓ Sentence 18

Name: ______________________________ Date: ________

38 Which sentence uses a helping verb with a main verb?

Ⓕ Sentence 6

Ⓖ Sentence 9

Ⓗ Sentence 10

Ⓘ Sentence 19

39 Which sentence uses a linking verb?

Ⓐ Sentence 1

Ⓑ Sentence 6

Ⓒ Sentence 11

Ⓓ Sentence 17

40 Which sentence has an error in subject-verb agreement?

Ⓕ Sentence 15

Ⓖ Sentence 16

Ⓗ Sentence 18

Ⓘ Sentence 19

STOP

Writing Prompt – Opinion Piece

The principal wants your class to build and manage a vegetable garden at your school. Think about whether this is a good idea or not.

Write an opinion paper to convince the principal to agree with your view about whether to have a garden.

Use the space below to plan your writing. Write your final copy on a clean sheet of paper.

Answer Key

Name: ____________________

Question	Correct Answer	Content Focus	CCSS	Complexity
1	C	Context Clues: Cause and Effect	L.5.4a	DOK 2
2	H	Context Clues: Sentence Clues	L.5.4a	DOK 2
3	A	Latin Roots	L.5.4b	DOK 1
4	H	Context Clues: Comparison	L.5.4a	DOK 2
5	B	Literary Element: Sensory Language	RI.5.1	DOK 2
6	I	Author's Point of View	RI.5.8	DOK 3
7	D	Main Idea and Key Details	RI.5.2	DOK 2
8	see below	Text Features: Use Illustrations	RI.4.7	DOK 2
9	B	Main Idea and Key Details	RI.5.2	DOK 2
10	see below	Main Idea and Key Details	RI.5.2	DOK 2
11	D	Context Clues: Sentence Clues	L.5.4a	DOK 2
12	G	Latin Roots	L.5.4b	DOK 1
13	C	Context Clues: Comparison	L.5.4a	DOK 2
14	H	Author's Point of View	RI.5.8	DOK 3
15	B	Main Idea and Key Details	RI.5.2	DOK 2
16	G	Personification	L.5.5a	DOK 2
17	see below	Author's Point of View	RI.5.8	DOK 3
18	F	Author's Point of View	RI.5.8	DOK 3
19	D	Main Idea and Key Details	RI.5.2	DOK 2
20	see below	Compare Across Texts	RI.5.9	DOK 4
21	B	Latin Roots	L.5.4b	DOK 1
22	G	Context Clues: Comparison	L.5.4a	DOK 2

Answer Key

Name: ____________________

Question	Correct Answer	Content Focus	CCSS	Complexity
23	C	Context Clues: Cause/Effect	L.5.4a	DOK 2
24	G	Literary Element: Personification	RL.5.4	DOK 2
25	A	Theme	RL.5.2	DOK 3
26	I	Theme	RL.5.2	DOK 3
27	B	Text Evidence	RL.5.1	DOK 3
28	see below	Text Evidence	RL.5.1	DOK 3
29	D	Literary Element: Sensory Language	RL.5.4	DOK 2
30	see below	Text Evidence	RL.5.1	DOK 3
31	C	Subject-Verb Agreement	L.3.1f	DOK 1
32	F	Action Verbs	L.3.1a	DOK 1
33	C	Verb Tenses	L.5.1d	DOK 1
34	G	Irregular Verbs	L.3.1d	DOK 1
35	B	Irregular Verbs	L.3.1d	DOK 1
36	G	Verb Tenses	L.4.1b	DOK 1
37	B	Verb Tenses	L.5.1b	DOK 1
38	H	Main Verbs and Helping Verbs	L.5.1	DOK 1
39	D	Linking Verbs	L.5.1	DOK 1
40	I	Linking Verbs	L.5.1	DOK 1
Prompt	see below	Opinion Writing	W.5.1a-d	DOK 3

Comprehension: Multiple-Choice 5, 6, 7, 9, 14, 15, 16, 18, 19, 24, 25, 26, 27, 29	/14	%
Comprehension: Constructed Response 8, 10, 17, 20, 28, 30	/16	%
Vocabulary 1, 2, 3, 4, 11, 12, 13, 21, 22, 23	/10	%
Grammar, Mechanics, Usage 31–40	/10	%
Total Unit Assessment Score	/50	%

Answer Key

Name: ______________________________

8 **2-point item.** The map shows the route of Ponce de León's voyage in 1513. It shows that he started in Puerto Rico, went north to the Bahamas, and then continued north to Florida, where he traveled along both coasts. He then went to Cuba and returned to Puerto Rico. It also shows that he made many stops along his voyage.

10 **2-point item.** Ponce de León was in conflict with the natives in the New World. He fought against and defeated natives on Hispaniola and Puerto Rico. He forced natives to mine gold in Puerto Rico. During a visit to Florida he was attacked, and he eventually died of a wound from a native arrow.

17 **2-point item.** Students should give evidence that supports the author's point of view that the Dosters are a brave family that could adapt to a new land. Examples: Many new settlers left soon after the Big Freeze of 1894, but the Doster family stayed. Slowly, Doster's wife and two daughters learned to love the land of southern Florida and respect its dangers. Dora's mother was a strong and brave woman.

20 **4-point item.** Students should note that Ponce de León came to the New World to discover and claim new lands, while the Dosters came to help a family member. Ponce de León was the first European to explore, claim, and settle lands such as Puerto Rico and Florida. Ponce de León was very successful in finding gold and became rich from it, but he was unable to establish a settlement in Florida or to find a fountain of youth (if he was searching for it). The Dosters experienced the beauty and dangers of a new area in the wilderness of Florida, and they were successful in helping Ben Doster's sister and making a new family home in Florida.

28 **2-point item.** Students should note that Lily has positive feelings about history by the end of the passage, while she had negative feelings in the beginning. They should note her belief that history is "boring" in the beginning, her interest in the photographs and journals as part of the class, and the fact that the hour seemed to fly by rather than crawl.

30 **4-point item.** Ms. Traynor uses local artifacts such as photos, letters, and journals to make a connection between the students and the people who moved there many years ago. By using these personal connections, Lily begins to see her own life is connected to people from earlier times and that she may have many of the same concerns at her age as people of earlier times did.

Writing Prompt

Refer to the scoring criteria in the Teacher Introduction to assess written responses to the prompt.

Read the passage and the play. Then answer the questions that follow.

Stormalong Disobeys an Order

Have you ever heard of Old Stormalong, the greatest sailor of all time? He was so strong that he could win an arm wrestling contest with an octopus with one arm tied behind his back. He was so tall that he used the ship's mast for a hat rack. And whenever the wind died down and becalmed the ship, Stormalong would take a seat at the stern and start whistling. With just one tune, he would puff out enough air to keep the ship sailing until the breeze picked up again. As you can imagine, ship captains loved having Stormalong aboard, even if it did require an extra supply room just to keep him fed.

When he was a lad, Stormalong was of course quite big for his age. He was also as curious as a monkey and as lively as a grasshopper. This was a challenging combination for his parents. They had to work hard to keep little Stormy out of mischief. Every day, they took him to the beach in hopes of wearing him out. Stormy would run up and down chasing seagulls. Scooping up sea creatures in his bucket, he would examine them awhile and then let them go. Most of the animals seemed okay with this. The giant squids, however, grew tired of the game and took off for the deepest parts of the ocean. They stayed there so long that folks started to doubt they really existed.

There are a lot of good yarns about Stormalong. One about his teenage years has Stormy and his friends doing "cannonballs" from a diving raft. They were trying to make the biggest splash. On Stormy's first turn, he leaped out over the water, hugged his knees to his chest, and curled his body into a ball. His splash was HUGE! In fact, the spray created the Great Lakes. The ripples formed the currents that still circle through the oceans today.

GO ON →

One of the best stories comes from the summer Stormy's parents signed him up for sailing lessons. He loved zipping through the water with the salt spray in his face. Ignoring his instructor's warnings about going too fast, he once crashed right into Africa. He hit the continent so hard that a piece broke off and formed Australia. Of course, his sailboat was destroyed. Luckily, Stormy was a true fish when it came to swimming. He just headed back across the ocean, using the opportunity to practice his crawl stroke. He arrived home in time for dinner and wasn't even tired.

When he was 18, Stormalong decided to become a sailor. He kissed his parents goodbye and set off for the nearest seaport. The captain saw him coming from two states away and signed him up before he even arrived. Though some in the crew were doubtful about his lack of experience, Stormalong promptly proved his worth.

Before the Panama Canal was built, ships traveling between the Atlantic and the Pacific had to sail around the tip of South America. It was a long and extremely dangerous journey. On his very first voyage, Stormalong's ship was set to sail that route. Stormalong had lookout duty. He spotted some bad weather, a huge storm near the Falkland Islands. Going through the storm would mean certain disaster for the ship. However, the first mate refused to tell the captain, who was asleep in his cabin. "You can't see the Falklands from here," he scoffed. "Get back to your post."

What could Stormalong do? Disobeying orders was a serious offense. He'd likely be severely punished. Even worse, he'd probably never get hired on a ship again. If he did obey the order, his shipmates might perish. Stormalong made his decision. He didn't go back to his post. Instead, he jumped overboard, picked up the vessel, hoisted it over Panama, and dropped it into the Pacific. The splash woke the captain. He was not angry at all about Stormalong taking matters into his own hands. In fact, he fired the first mate and offered Stormalong the job. (He also began promoting the idea of a canal across Panama.)

Saving that ship made Stormalong an instant legend. People still tell stories about him to this day.

GO ON →

The Poet and the General

CHARACTERS

NARRATOR	
JOHN WHEATLEY	wealthy merchant, white, age 58
YOUNG PHILLIS	girl, black, age 7
MARY WHEATLEY	John's daughter, white, age 18
PHILLIS WHEATLEY	woman, black, age 23
GEORGE WASHINGTON	man, white, age 44
OFFICER	man, any age

SCENE 1

NARRATOR *(Spotlighted on dark stage)* In October 1775, early in the Revolutionary War, a young woman named Phillis Wheatley sent a poem to General George Washington. In a letter dated February 28, 1776, Washington invited Wheatley, who lived in Boston, Massachusetts, to visit him at his headquarters in nearby Cambridge. She reportedly did so in March 1776, but no one knows for sure. The poet and the general—what might such a meeting have been like?

Walks offstage. The light dims…

SCENE 2

Setting: The parlor of the Wheatley home in Boston, 1761.
Mary Wheatley is sitting and sewing when John Wheatley and Young Phillis enter from the left.

JOHN WHEATLEY Mary, this slave child has just arrived from Africa aboard Captain Fitch's vessel. I bought her to be a servant and companion to your mother. She speaks no English but seems very intelligent and quick to learn. Perhaps you can teach her?

GO ON →

MARY WHEATLEY I will happily do so, Father. What is the child's name?

JOHN WHEATLEY She is called Phillis, after the ship on which she arrived.

MARY WHEATLEY Phillis—Phillis Wheatley. It's a good name. Come with me, Phillis Wheatley.

She takes the child's hand and leads her from the room. The lights dim.

SCENE 3

Setting: The dining room of a house, March 1776. General Washington sips a cup of tea and examines some papers on the table. There is a knock at the door.

OFFICER (From offstage.) General Washington, Phillis Wheatley has arrived.

Phillis Wheatley now age 23, enters from the right. General Washington stands and gestures for her to sit, then takes his seat.

WASHINGTON You are a remarkable woman, Mistress Wheatley. I am flattered you have chosen me as the subject of one of your poems, though I would quarrel with the title: "His Excellency George Washington." I am no "Excellency"—just a man serving his country.

WHEATLEY I meant no offense, sir. The title merely reflects the judgments I hear spoken all around me. Your fellow citizens think very highly of you, General.

WASHINGTON I wonder what the state of their opinion will be as this war with England continues. They may feel I have led them out of the frying pan into the fire.

GO ON →

WHEATLEY — Sir, all praise is rightly deserved. Your past achievements—your bravery, honesty, manners, intelligence—are well known. They are the reason the people confidently call on you to lead the brave troops who protect us and gain us our freedom from English tyrants.

WASHINGTON — You say the same in your poem. I thank you for those elegant words. But I am curious, how did you come to write poetry? How were you educated?

WHEATLEY — After I learned English, Mary Wheatley taught me to read and write. Since the age of 12, I have been reading English and Latin poets. The Wheatleys have always encouraged me. They even help me publish my poems.

WASHINGTON — Ah, yes, I have seen your book, *Poems on Various Subjects, Religious and Moral*. I understand that yours is only the second book published by a woman from the American colonies. That is quite an achievement for any person so young, and especially one who has lived in enslavement. (*Stands*) I am honored to have met you, Mistress Wheatley, but I regret I must now return to my work.

WHEATLEY — (*rises and curtseys*) General, you have many unencouraging days ahead. When times are hardest, take comfort in the saying that "the hour is darkest before the dawn."

WASHINGTON — You have succeeded in rising above the tyranny of slavery. That gives me great hope in our struggle with the tyranny of England.

Washington grasps Wheatley's hand in both of his. The lights dim.

GO ON →

Name: ______________________________ Date: ________

Use "Stormalong Disobeys an Order" on pages 81 and 82 to answer Numbers 1 through 10.

1 Who is the narrator of this passage?

Ⓐ someone who is not part of the story

Ⓑ one of Stormalong's teenage friends

Ⓒ one of Stormalong's parents

Ⓓ a member of the ship's crew

2 What makes Stormalong a tall tale hero? Use clear text evidence from the story to support your answer.

____

____

____

____

____

____

GO ON →

Name: ______________________________ Date: __________

3 Read this sentence from the passage.

He was also as curious as a monkey and as lively as a grasshopper.

Using clear text evidence, explain why the author compares Stormalong to a monkey and a grasshopper. Then choose a detail from the story supporting each comparison.

____

____

____

____

____

____

4 Read this sentence from the passage.

With just one tune, he would puff out enough air to keep the ship sailing until the breeze picked up again.

What mood does the author create by using this kind of exaggeration?

Ⓕ amusement

Ⓖ fear

Ⓗ scorn

Ⓘ suspense

GO ON →

Name: ______________________________ Date: ________

5 Read this sentence from the passage.

Ignoring his instructor's warnings about going too fast, he once crashed right into Africa.

If *instruct* means "teach," what does *instructor* mean?

Ⓐ something that is taught

Ⓑ a person who teaches

Ⓒ the act of teaching

Ⓓ teach again

6 Read this sentence from the passage.

Luckily, Stormy was a true fish when it came to swimming.

What does *Stormy was a true fish* mean in this sentence?

Ⓕ Stormy used fins to swim with.

Ⓖ Stormy was a very skillful swimmer.

Ⓗ Stormy learned to swim by observing fish.

Ⓘ Stormy could swim underwater for a long time.

7 Which of the following details from the passage is an example of hyperbole?

Ⓐ Stormalong's parents had to work hard to keep him out of mischief.

Ⓑ Stormy's cannonball splash created the Great Lakes and ocean currents.

Ⓒ Sailing around the tip of South America was a long and extremely dangerous journey.

Ⓓ Stormalong kissed his parents goodbye and set off for the nearest seaport.

GO ON →

Name: ______________________________ Date: ________

8 Based on clear text evidence, what message does the author want to get across in the last three paragraphs?

Ⓕ If you want to be remembered, do something brave.

Ⓖ People who disobey their leaders should be punished.

Ⓗ Sometimes disobeying an order is the right thing to do.

Ⓘ Leaders must be careful in making important decisions.

9 Which sentence best describes the hero of the story as a boy?

Ⓐ He does not understand why the giant squids are afraid of him.

Ⓑ He thinks it's funny when his actions make big changes in the landscape.

Ⓒ His great size and strength are always getting him into trouble with his parents.

Ⓓ His activities are like those of many other kids, but the results are not ordinary.

10 The narrator of this story seems to find Stormalong entertaining. Which statement below supports this claim or view based on clear text evidence?

Ⓕ describes how Stormalong's parents felt

Ⓖ says Stormalong was very strong

Ⓗ talks about Stormalong as if he were a real person

Ⓘ enjoys sharing stories about Stormalong

GO ON →

Name: ______________________________ Date: ________

Use "The Poet and the General" on pages 83–85 to answer Numbers 11 through 19.

11 What text evidence best tells the message of this play?

Ⓐ "You have succeeded in rising above the tyranny of slavery."

Ⓑ "I bought her to be a servant and companion to your mother."

Ⓒ "After I learned English, Mary Wheatley taught me to read and write."

Ⓓ "Ah, yes, I have seen your book, *Poems on Various Subjects, Religious and Moral*."

12 How does the use of a narrator help the reader better understand the play?

Ⓕ The narrator provides details that the characters would not know.

Ⓖ The narrator supplies some historical background for the play.

Ⓗ The narrator summarizes the main events of the play.

Ⓘ The narrator reveals the author's point of view.

13 Explain how the list and descriptions of the characters on page 83 add to the reader's understanding of the play. Support your answer with clear text evidence.

____

____

____

____

____

____

GO ON →

Name: ______________________ Date: ________

14 Read this sentence from the play.

They may feel I have led them out of the frying pan into the fire.

What does the saying *out of the frying pan into the fire* mean?

Ⓕ from the kitchen into another room

Ⓖ from a place of safety into a place of danger

Ⓗ from one bad situation into a worse situation

Ⓘ from an uncertainty into a definite course of action

15 Scene 2 is important for understanding the rest of the play because the reader

Ⓐ learns about Phillis Wheatley's background.

Ⓑ is introduced to Captain Fitch, a main character.

Ⓒ comes to find out about Washington's love of poetry.

Ⓓ is made aware of the effects of war on enslaved people.

16 Read this sentence from the play.

General, you have many unencouraging days ahead.

What does *unencouraging* mean?

Ⓕ in an encouraging way

Ⓖ encouraging again

Ⓗ not encouraging

Ⓘ too encouraging

GO ON →

Name: ______________________________ Date: ________

17 Read this sentence from the play.

When times are hardest, I hope you may take comfort in the saying that "the hour is darkest before the dawn."

What does *the hour is darkest before the dawn* mean?

Ⓐ You can defeat the enemy by attacking early in the morning.

Ⓑ Even though things seem hopeless, success is near.

Ⓒ The sunrise is brightest after the moon goes down.

Ⓓ Victory is never possible without a fight.

18 How does the author signal that a scene is ending?

Ⓕ by dimming the lights

Ⓖ by closing the stage curtain

Ⓗ by having the narrator speak

Ⓘ by having a character enter the stage

19 Which statement best supports George Washington's opinion that Phillis Wheatley is "a remarkable woman?"

Ⓐ She began reading Latin poetry when she was only 12.

Ⓑ She believed Washington would be a great leader.

Ⓒ She arrived in America as a small child.

Ⓓ She was named after a ship.

GO ON →

Name: ______________________ Date: ________

Use "Stormalong Disobeys an Order" and "The Poet and the General" to answer the question below.

20 Compare and contrast Phillis Wheatley's view of George Washington with the tall tale narrator's view of Stormalong. Include what their opinions are based on and how they are expressed. Support your answer with clear text evidence from the two selections.

GO ON →

Read the article "Learning from Folk Medicine" before answering Numbers 21 through 30.

Learning from Folk Medicine

Today, when we are sick, we can go to a doctor for treatment. Doctors have found cures and treatments for many diseases. Modern medicine has been extremely valuable to humanity. It has helped people survive serious diseases and suffer less pain.

Before modern medicine, people also had ways to help those who were sick. They turned to nature to find cures. They discovered plants that could be used to heal or treat illnesses. When they found something that worked, they would share the remedy with others. This information was passed down from one generation to another. It is often called folk medicine.

Many people think that we can't learn anything from folk medicine. But that is not true. You might be surprised to find out how many modern medicines are based on old folk remedies.

Many folk remedies used tree bark as an ingredient. The native peoples of Canada and the United States used the bark of the chokecherry tree to treat colds and coughs. After they removed the bark from the tree, they would dry it, then boil the proper amount and make a tea. The tea tasted good and made people feel better. Modern scientists discovered that the tea does soothe people's sore throats. It also allows the person to heal more swiftly because of the nutrients it contains. Nowadays the bark is used as a flavoring in some cough syrups.

GO ON →

Malaria is a deadly disease in some countries. Long ago, the Inca of South America found a way to treat malaria. They made a medicine using the bark of the cinchona tree. In the 1600s, Spanish explorers were surprised to see the Incan people using cinchona powder to treat malaria effectively. Later, the Spanish sent the powder to other regions where the disease was also a problem. People in other areas also successfully used the powder. Cinchona powder was used for over 200 years before a scientist studied it. He realized that a specific chemical in the tree bark helped fight the disease. The chemical was named quinine after the Incan word for "tree bark." Quinine is still used today to treat malaria.

The Japanese have known for hundreds of years that eating a type of red seaweed would help them with intestinal problems. Not long ago, scientists discovered that this red seaweed contains kainic acid, which can be used in medicine. The medicine is used to get rid of parasites in the intestines.

The Incan people used cinchona powder, which contains quinine, to treat malaria.

GO ON →

For centuries, traditional healers in the British Isles used a flowering plant called foxglove to treat ulcers, bruises, and other problems. One of its main uses was for edema, or the buildup of fluid in the body. An 18th-century English doctor showed that this problem was often associated with heart failure and that foxglove had a positive effect on the heart muscle. (However, it is highly poisonous in the wrong doses.) Today, a drug called *digitalis* is made from foxglove leaves. The drug is prescribed for people with certain heart problems.

People are often quick to reject or ignore ideas from the past. They don't think we can learn anything from folk medicine. But as these examples show, we shouldn't ignore old ideas. Scientists can base new medicines on old remedies. Scientists are still researching some of the plants and other ingredients used in folk medicine. Who knows what old remedy will become a new medicine?

Plant	Use in Folk Medicine	Modern Use
chokecherry bark	colds and coughs	Bark is used to make cough syrup flavoring.
cinchona bark	malaria	Quinine (chemical in the bark) is used to treat malaria.
red seaweed	intestinal problems	Kainic acid (in red seaweed) kills intestinal parasites.
foxglove leaves	edema	Digitalis (made from the leaves) affects the heart muscle and helps with certain heart diseases.

GO ON →

Name: ______________________________ Date: ________

Now answer Numbers 21 through 30. Base your answers on "Learning from Folk Medicine."

21 Read this sentence from the article.

Modern medicine has been extremely valuable to humanity.

Which sentence from the article supports this idea?

Ⓐ Cinchona powder was used for over 200 years before a scientist studied it.

Ⓑ Nowadays the bark is used as a flavoring in some cough syrups.

Ⓒ Doctors have found cures and treatments for many diseases.

Ⓓ Malaria is a deadly disease in some countries.

22 What would be a good title for the chart in this article?

Ⓕ How Folk Medicine and Modern Medicine Are Different

Ⓖ Examples of Folk Medicines with Modern Uses

Ⓗ Substances for Making Tea

Ⓘ Trees Doctors Can Use

23 In the chart, what do the words in bold type tell you?

Ⓐ what kind of information is in each column

Ⓑ the plants used to make folk medicines

Ⓒ how the information is linked to the article

Ⓓ the most important terms from the article

GO ON →

Name: ______________________ Date: __________

24 What is the author's view of folk medicines? Use clear text evidence to explain how the author supports this view.

____

____

____

____

____

____

25 Read these sentences from the article.

They discovered plants that could be used to heal or treat illnesses. When they found something that worked, they would share the remedy with others.

What words tell you what *remedy* means?

Ⓐ discovered plants

Ⓑ to heal or treat

Ⓒ found something

Ⓓ with others

26 Which words from the article have almost the same meaning?

Ⓕ *information* and *nature*

Ⓖ *traditional* and *modern*

Ⓗ *illnesses* and *diseases*

Ⓘ *nutrients* and *amount*

GO ON →

Name: ______________________________ Date: ________

27 Read this sentence from the article.

One of its main uses was for edema, or the buildup of fluid in the body.

If a person had *edema* in his or her ankle, the ankle would appear to be

Ⓐ bruised.

Ⓑ fragile.

Ⓒ painful.

Ⓓ swollen.

28 What is the purpose of the picture and caption on page 95?

Ⓕ to describe how folk healers used cinchona

Ⓖ to show how the Spanish learned about cinchona

Ⓗ to help the reader understand the author's viewpoint

Ⓘ to give an example of a folk medicine that can be dangerous

29 Read this sentence from the article.

People are often quick to reject or ignore ideas from the past.

Which word has the OPPOSITE meaning of *reject?*

Ⓐ accept

Ⓑ deny

Ⓒ learn

Ⓓ question

GO ON →

Name: ______________________________ Date: __________

30 Read the paragraph below.

In the United States, new medicines must go through a long series of laboratory tests before they can be sold. They must also be tried on volunteer patients. This process helps to ensure the medicine is safe and actually works. But these steps should not be required for folk medicines. After all, traditional treatments are not new. They have already been tested over many years on thousands of people.

How does the point of view expressed in this paragraph compare with the author's point of view in "Learning from Folk Medicine"? Support your answer with clear text evidence.

____

____

____

____

____

____

____

____

____

____

____

____

____

____

____

____

GO ON →

Read the article below. Choose the answer that correctly completes questions 31–40.

Dolley Payne Todd Madison (1768–1849) was not the first First Lady, but she ___(31)___ the first to take on many of the roles that First Ladies still play today. ___(32)___ husband James was the fourth president of the United States. Throughout Madison's time in office, Dolley worked hard to make foreign officials feel welcome in the White House. She wanted to show ___(33)___ that we Americans were not rough country folk. Our education and manners were equal to ___(34)___ in Europe. Social events also gave Dolley the chance to help her husband with his job. She used them to gain information that might be useful. She even persuaded some guests to change ___(35)___ views of Madison's policies.

Modern First Ladies often dedicate ___(36)___ to particular public projects. They ___(37)___ programs to support literacy, for example, or improve the nation's health. Dolley Madison was the first to do this. She organized a home for orphan girls in Washington, D.C., and donated food for ___(38)___ kitchen.

During the War of 1812, the British army burned the White House. Dolley refused to leave without a large portrait of George Washington, ___(39)___ hung in the State Dining Room. This was a very patriotic act. Fortunately, no other First Lady has needed to repeat ___(40)___!

GO ON →

Name: ______________________________ Date: ________

31 Which answer should go in blank (31)?

Ⓐ were

Ⓑ was

Ⓒ are

32 Which answer should go in blank (32)?

Ⓕ She's

Ⓖ Hers

Ⓗ Her

33 Which answer should go in blank (33)?

Ⓐ her

Ⓑ him

Ⓒ them

34 Which answer should go in blank (34)?

Ⓕ anyones

Ⓖ anyone's

Ⓗ anyones'

35 Which answer should go in blank (35)?

Ⓐ their

Ⓑ there

Ⓒ they're

GO ON →

Name: ______________________ Date: ________

36 Which answer should go in blank (36)?

Ⓕ theirself

Ⓖ themselfs

Ⓗ themselves

37 Which answer should go in blank (37)?

Ⓐ start

Ⓑ starts

Ⓒ starting

38 Which answer should go in blank (38)?

Ⓕ it's

Ⓖ its

Ⓗ its's

39 Which answer should go in blank (39)?

Ⓐ that

Ⓑ who

Ⓒ which

40 Which answer should go in blank (40)?

Ⓕ it

Ⓖ them

Ⓗ those

STOP

Writing Prompt – Narrative

Think about a time when you or someone you know had to make an important decision or choice.

Write a narrative, or a story, telling what happened, what decision or choice had to be made, and how it was made.

Use the space below to plan your writing. Write your narrative on a separate sheet of paper.

Answer Key

Name: ______________________

Question	Correct Answer	Content Focus	CCSS	Complexity
1	A	Point of View	RL.5.6	DOK 3
2	See below	Literary Elements: Hero	RL.5.1	DOK 3
3	See below	Simile	L.5.5a	DOK 2
4	F	Literary Elements: Hyperbole	RL.5.4	DOK 2
5	B	Suffixes	L.5.4	DOK 1
6	G	Metaphor	L.5.5a	DOK 2
7	B	Literary Elements: Hyperbole	RL.5.4	DOK 2
8	H	Theme	RL.5.2	DOK 3
9	D	Literary Elements: Hero	RL.5.1	DOK 3
10	I	Point of View	RL 5.6	DOK 3
11	A	Theme	RL.5.2	DOK 3
12	G	Point of View	RL 5.6	DOK 3
13	See below	Literary Elements	RL.4.7	DOK 2
14	H	Adages and Proverbs	L.5.5b	DOK 2
15	A	Literary Elements: Scenes	RL.5.5	DOK 3
16	H	Prefixes	L.5.4	DOK 1
17	B	Adages and Proverbs	L.5.5b	DOK 2
18	F	Literary Elements: Scenes	RL.5.5	DOK 2
19	A	Point of View	RL.5.6	DOK 3
20	See below	Compare Across Texts	RL.5.9	DOK 4
21	C	Author's Point of View	RI.5.8	DOK 3
22	G	Text Features: Chart	RI.4.7	DOK 2

Answer Key

Name: ____________________

Question	Answer	Content Focus	CCSS	Complexity
23	A	Text Features: Chart	RI.4.7	DOK 1
24	See below	Author's Point of View	RI.5.8	DOK 3
25	B	Context Clues: Definitions and Restatements	L.5.4a	DOK 2
26	H	Synonyms	L.5.5c	DOK 1
27	D	Context Clues: Definitions and Restatements	L.5.4a	DOK 2
28	G	Text Features: Photos and Illustrations	RI.4.7	DOK 1
29	A	Antonyms	L.5.5c	DOK 1
30	See below	Author's Point of View	RI.5.8	DOK 3
31	B	Pronoun-Verb Agreement	L.3.1f	DOK 1
32	H	Possessive Pronouns	L.5.1	DOK 1
33	C	Pronouns and Antecedents	L.3.1f	DOK 1
34	G	Possessive Pronouns	L.5.2	DOK 1
35	A	Pronouns and Homophones	L.4.1g	DOK 1
36	H	Kinds of Pronouns	L.3.1a	DOK 1
37	A	Pronoun-Verb Agreement	L.3.1f	DOK 1
38	G	Pronouns and Homophones	L.4.1g	DOK 1
39	C	Kinds of Pronouns	L.3.1a	DOK 1
40	F	Pronouns and Antecedents	L.3.1f	DOK 1
Prompt	See below	Narrative Writing	W.5.3 a-e	DOK 3

Comprehension: Multiple-Choice 1, 4, 6, 7, 10, 12, 14, 15, 16, 17, 21, 22, 23, 28	/14	%
Comprehension: Constructed Response 2, 3, 13, 20, 24, 30	/16	%
Vocabulary 5, 8, 9, 11, 18, 19, 25, 26, 27, 29	/10	%
Grammar, Mechanics, Usage 31–40	/10	%
Total Unit Assessment Score	/50	%

Answer Key

Name: ______________________

2 **2-point item.** Responses should show awareness that tall tale heroes are usually exaggerated. Stormalong is extremely big and strong. He does amazing things that real people cannot do. His actions and their consequences go far beyond what could happen in real life.

3 **2-point item.** "As curious as a monkey" suggests that Stormalong wants to investigate whatever he comes in contact with, especially in a hands-on way. An example is Stormy scooping up sea creatures to look at them. "As lively as a grasshopper" suggests that Stormalong is very active and full of restless energy. Examples include Stormy running up and down the beach and sailing his sailboat very fast.

13 **2-point item.** The names and descriptions of characters acquaint the reader with the people that appear in the play. In this way, the reader can visualize Wheatley, Washington, and others before the play begins.

20 **4-point item.** Responses should be in paragraph form and should include both similarities and differences in the two viewpoints. **Sample similarities:** Wheatley and the narrator both admire their subjects (but in different ways). Both base their opinions at least in part on what other people have said. Both use special names for the subject that reflect their feelings (His Excellency, Sir, Old Stormalong, Stormy). Both refer to the subject's past achievements. **Sample differences:** Wheatley respects Washington, while the narrator is amused by Stormalong. Wheatley speaks only of Washington's successes, while the narrator includes Stormalong's mishaps as well. Wheatley expresses her admiration in written form (poem) and in person; the narrator's feelings come through indirectly during the narrative. Wheatley speaks in general terms but does not describe actual deeds or events; the narrator describes specific episodes.

24 **2-point item.** The author thinks there is great value in some folk medicines. The author tells stories of some folk medicines that worked very well and points out that many modern medicines are based on old folk remedies.

30 **4-point item.** Responses should be in paragraph form and should indicate that the article's author would likely disagree with the paragraph's main argument, that scientific testing should not be required for folk medicines. While the article shows respect and open-mindedness toward folk treatments, it also clearly values science. The author sees value in learning from folk remedies and modifying them as appropriate, but he or she does not support the idea of adopting all folk medicines without researching and understanding why they work.

Writing Prompt

Refer to the scoring criteria in the Teacher Introduction to assess written responses to the prompt.

Exploring Mammoth Cave

Today, most visitors enter the caves at Mammoth Cave National Park in Kentucky through a well-lit walkway. About 390 miles of connecting passages have been explored there. Scientists estimate there may be 600 more miles to go!

Mammoth Cave was probably discovered by Native Americans about 4,000 years ago. Native American miners collected crystals from it. White settlers discovered the entrance in the 1790s. In the early 1800s, slaves worked in the caves to mine saltpeter. This mineral was used in making gunpowder during the War of 1812.

Three Young Explorers

In 1838, Franklin Gorin bought the property containing the cave mouth. He had plans to turn it into a tourist attraction. He worked to build a hotel near the entrance and turned over the exploration of the cave to three teenage slaves named Stephen Bishop, Mat Bransford, and Nick Bransford. A doctor named John Croghan bought the land and took ownership of the slaves the next year. At one time, Croghan treated patients at a special hospital inside the cave.

The three young men who explored the cave had only candles and lanterns for light. They were the first to explore many miles of caves. First, they had to get across the Bottomless Pit. It was a deep, black hole like a giant mouth that blocked one passage. Stephen crossed it by laying down a ladder and crawling over. They gave a name to each new wonder they found. They named passageways, such as Grand Avenue, and rock formations, such as a giant stone column called The Devil's Armchair. A large, open room was named The Church.

When they explored a new area, they often carved their names into a rocky wall. Sometimes they wrote their names on the ceiling using smoke from a candle. Many of these marks still survive. They show that the young slaves' outlook was similar to that of some modern cave explorers. They were willing to take great risks to discover what others had never seen.

GO ON →

Cave Tours

These young men gave day-long tours to people from all over the world. Some visitors stayed as long as a week. By exploring and talking with visitors who knew about caves, the young men became familiar with the geology of the cave. They knew how the cave was formed, and they learned the different types of rocks.

On some tours, visitors had to crawl on their hands and knees through a passage for more than 20 feet. Other tours included a boat ride down an underground river. Tourists had to lie down flat in the boat to pass beneath a low ceiling. The guides delighted in giving visitors a chance to "try the dark." That meant leaving the visitors for a few minutes in the pitch black of the caverns. Soon afterward, they led the visitors to the Star Chamber. When they looked up at the ceiling, it seemed that stars were glittering in a night sky.

The young men showed visitors the strange fish and shrimp living in the cave's waters. Some were completely white, and most had no eyes. They did not need eyes since there was never any light to help them see. The guides sometimes sold these fish to tourists to earn money.

All of the guides hoped to buy their freedom one day. Stephen Bishop was the first; he was able to buy his freedom from his owner in 1856. He planned to move to Liberia in Africa, but he died the next year. Nick Bransford managed to buy his way out of slavery in 1863, but Mat was not so lucky. Before the end of the Civil War in 1865, his wife's owner had sold three of their four children.

U.S. National Park Service

Both Nick and Mat stayed near the natural wonder they had explored. They gave tours for many years. The next generations of Bransfords, as well as many other African Americans, gave tours until the 1930s when the U.S. National Park Service took over. The Mammoth Cave National Park officially opened in 1941. Then, in 2006, a fifth-generation member of the Bransford family began to give tours through the caverns. He was following in the footsteps of his ancestors.

GO ON →

Today, more than 2 million people visit Mammoth Cave every year. The U.S. National Park Service offers many different tours. Some of the tours follow the same routes that Stephen Bishop and the Bransfords took in the 1800s.

Popular Mammoth Cave Tours					
Name	**Highlights**	**Distance**	**Time**	**Elevation Change**	**Difficulty**
Grand Avenue	Snowball Room, Thorpe's Pit, Frozen Niagara	4 miles	$4\frac{1}{2}$ hr	280 ft	Strenuous
Historic	Historic entrance, Bottomless Pit, Mammoth Dome	2 miles	2 hr	300 ft	Moderate
Mammoth Passage	Largest rooms, early mining operations	$\frac{3}{4}$ mile	$1\frac{1}{4}$ hr	160 ft	Easy
River Styx	Underground rivers and Lake Lethe	$2\frac{1}{2}$ miles	$2\frac{1}{2}$ hr	360 ft	Moderate
Star Chamber	Star Chamber, John Croghan's hospital	$1\frac{1}{2}$ miles	$2\frac{1}{2}$ hr	160 ft	Moderate
Wild Cave	Crawling through caves with headlamps	5 miles	6 hr	300 ft	Very Difficult

GO ON →

Name: ______________________________ Date: ________

Use "A Spelunking Trip" on pages 108 and 109 to answer Numbers 1 through 10.

1. Read this sentence from the passage.

   The class congregated around the entrance.

   The root of *congregated* is a Latin word meaning "to flock together." What is the most likely meaning of *congregated*?

   Ⓐ gathered

   Ⓑ pushed

   Ⓒ laughed and shouted

   Ⓓ raced around quickly

2. Read this sentence from the passage.

   "But the rules protect you from harm so you aren't vulnerable to it."

   What does *vulnerable* mean in the sentence above?

   Ⓕ beautiful

   Ⓖ delayed

   Ⓗ exposed

   Ⓘ understandable

3. Read these sentences from the passage.

   They were anxious to see what was in store. Two of the students, Karen and Tranh, started to duck into the cave.

   What does the idiom "in store" mean?

   Ⓐ for sale

   Ⓑ on the shelf

   Ⓒ about to happen

   Ⓓ outside the cave

GO ON →

Name: ______________________________ Date: ________

4 Read this sentence from the passage.

"Inside, we will want to learn as much as possible about the cave's ecology."

The word *ecology* comes from two Greek roots that mean "house or home" and "study." Knowing this suggests that studying the cave's *ecology* would involve learning about

Ⓕ people who study caves.

Ⓖ life that exists in the cave.

Ⓗ how long the cave has existed.

Ⓘ the dangers of exploring caves.

5 Read this sentence from the passage.

The crickets were as pale as ghosts and had longer legs and antennae than the cricket Marcie had found earlier.

What does "as pale as ghosts" mean?

Ⓐ The crickets were dead.

Ⓑ The crickets could not see.

Ⓒ The crickets were almost white.

Ⓓ The crickets made weird, spooky noises.

6 With which of these statements would the narrator of this passage be most likely to agree?

Ⓕ Caves are interesting, but there is not much to learn from them.

Ⓖ Ms. Odom should have done more to get the students interested in caves.

Ⓗ Spelunking is dangerous, even for the well-prepared.

Ⓘ A trip to a cave is exciting, and students can learn a lot.

GO ON →

Name: ______________________________ Date: ________

7. How are Karen and Tranh like the other students in the group, and how are they different? Use details from the passage in your answer.

____

____

____

____

____

____

8. How do Mammoth Cave's "twilight zone" and "dark zone" differ in detail?

Ⓕ The "dark zone" lies at the cave entrance; the "twilight zone" lies deeper in the cave.

Ⓖ Animal life is found in the "twilight zone" but none in the "dark zone."

Ⓗ Visitors use flashlights in the "dark zone" but not in the "twilight zone."

Ⓘ The "twilight zone" has yellow and brown cave crickets; the "dark zone" has white, eyeless crayfish.

GO ON →

Name: ______________________________ Date: ________

9 What does Marcie do that is different from the other students?

Ⓐ She follows the rules at all times.

Ⓑ She records her field notes outside the cave.

Ⓒ She notices more things about creatures in the cave.

Ⓓ She sees something fascinating everywhere she looks.

10 How are the students in Ms. Odom's class like real spelunkers, and how are they different? Use details from the passage to support your answer.

____

____

____

____

____

____

GO ON →

Name: ______________________________ Date: ________

Use "Exploring Mammoth Cave" on pages 110–112 to answer Numbers 11 through 20.

11 Read these sentences from the article.

Then, in 2006, a fifth-generation member of the Bransford family began to give tours through the caverns. He was following in the footsteps of his ancestors.

What does "following in the footsteps" mean in the sentences above?

Ⓐ following directions

Ⓑ wearing the same shoes

Ⓒ walking very quietly

Ⓓ doing the same thing

12 Read these sentences from the article.

They show that the young slaves' outlook was similar to that of some modern cave explorers. They were willing to take great risks to discover what others had never seen.

What does *outlook* mean in the sentences above?

Ⓕ a person's thoughts

Ⓖ knowledge or experience

Ⓗ tools used by explorers

Ⓘ ability to bear hardship

13 What is the purpose of the chart at the end of the article?

Ⓐ to explain why the Bransfords loved Mammoth Cave

Ⓑ to give an idea about the character of the early guides

Ⓒ to describe some of the tours people can take

Ⓓ to show what Mammoth Cave looks like

GO ON →

Name: ______________________________ Date: ________

14 Read these sentences from the article.

By exploring and talking with visitors who knew about caves, the young men became familiar with the geology of the cave. They knew how the cave was formed, and they learned the different types of rocks.

Which detail in the sentences helps the reader understand what *geology* means?

Ⓕ young men

Ⓖ visitors who knew

Ⓗ exploring and talking

Ⓘ how the cave was formed

15 Read these sentences from the article.

First, they had to get across the Bottomless Pit. It was a deep, black hole like a giant mouth that blocked one passage.

What effect is created by the simile in the sentences above?

Ⓐ It makes exploring the cave seem scary.

Ⓑ It makes the explorers seem happy and excited.

Ⓒ It makes the Bottomless Pit seem small and pleasant.

Ⓓ It makes the explorers seem unskillful.

16 With which of the following statements would the author most likely agree?

Ⓕ Mammoth Cave should not be a tourist destination.

Ⓖ Star Chamber is the most beautiful spot in the cave.

Ⓗ Early guides were important to the cave's exploration.

Ⓘ It would have been better for tourists if the early guides had been educated in college.

GO ON →

Name: ______________________________ Date: ________

17 According to the chart, which tour of Mammoth Cave is most difficult, and which is easiest? Use details from the chart to explain.

____

____

____

____

____

____

GO ON →

Name: ______________________________ Date: ______

18 What does the writer suggest the guides did with the money they earned from the sale of fish?

Ⓕ The money was given to the poor.

Ⓖ The guides used the money to pay taxes.

Ⓗ The money was used to buy new clothes.

Ⓘ The guides used the money to buy their freedom.

19 What evidence from the text shows that the author gives a lot of credit to the three young men who first explored Mammoth Cave?

Ⓐ The young men sold fish without eyes to some of the tourists.

Ⓑ The young men left visitors for a few minutes in the pitch black.

Ⓒ The young men were willing to take great risks to discover what others had never seen.

Ⓓ The young men treated patients at a special hospital inside the cave.

GO ON →

Name: ______________________ Date: ________

Use "A Spelunking Trip" and "Exploring Mammoth Cave" to answer the question below.

20 Both the students in Ms. Odom's class and the early guides of Mammoth Cave entered caves to make new discoveries. Compare and contrast their experiences and the conditions they faced. Use clear text evidence to support your answer.

GO ON →

Going to the Doctor

If you go to a doctor's office today, the doctor will usually know the cause of your illness and how to treat it. That was not true of doctors 200 years ago. No matter what symptoms you had, the treatment would be the same. Doctors did the best they could with what they knew at the time, but their knowledge was limited. The practice of medicine has changed a lot since then, both in understanding what causes diseases and knowing how to treat them.

In the 1700s, doctors believed that people's bodies held four liquids called "humors." These liquids reflected the elements of the natural world: air, water, earth, and fire. The four humors had to be balanced for a person to be healthy. One of the four was blood. Doctors believed that a person who had too much "bad blood" would become sick. The best way to keep people healthy or to cure a problem was to get rid of the bad blood.

For hundreds of years, doctors used bloodletting to treat patients with any number of problems, from fevers to back pain to broken bones. To remove the "bad blood," a doctor made a small cut in an arm or near a wound. The doctor then collected some amount of blood in a bowl. In most cases, the doctor would continue the bleeding until the patient was close to passing out. People believed this would get rid of the bad blood so that the patient's body could become balanced again.

Bloodletting was so common that doctors bought fancy pouches and kits to carry with them. These kits contained special tools for making small cuts. But people who didn't want to go to the doctor for bloodletting could go to a barber instead. Barbers performed the same procedure on healthy people to help them stay healthy. The usual sign for a barber shop was a red and white striped pole. Red represented blood, and white was for the bandages used to stop the bleeding.

GO ON →

George Washington died in 1799 from what modern doctors think was a throat infection. Like most people at the time, he believed in bloodletting. He asked to be bled when he first got sick. Later, doctors removed a lot of blood from his body. They hoped it would cure him. but it did not. He died 24 hours later. Bloodletting probably did not kill him, but it certainly did not help him recover.

If a person in the early 1800s was injured, a doctor might perform surgery. This might include removing an arm or leg that could not be saved or removing a bullet or another object. In those days, more people died from surgery than were saved.

One of the reasons so many people died was that doctors did not know about bacteria. They did not clean the germs from their hands or tools after working on one patient and beginning on another. Many patients got infections and died, but doctors did not understand why.

A British surgeon, Joseph Lister, showed in 1867 that careful cleaning between patients could greatly reduce the risk of infections. But American doctors were slow to accept his views. It was the treatment of another American president that helped change their minds.

In 1881, President James Garfield was shot as he entered a train station. Doctors worked on Garfield to try to remove the bullet. But they did not clean their hands or tools. They tended him in the same way for about 10 weeks before he died. Doctors found that he died from infection rather than the bullet. That discovery helped bring about some important changes in medicine.

Today's doctors know much more than they did in the past and use the best information available. We are lucky that modern medicine is as advanced as it is and offers so many benefits. Even so, some of their methods may change someday, too, as scientists make new discoveries.

GO ON →

Name: ______________________________ Date: ________

Now answer Numbers 21 through 30. Base your answers on "Going to the Doctor."

21 Read these sentences from the article.

> **If you go to a doctor's office today, the doctor will usually know the cause of your illness and how to treat it. That was not true of doctors 200 years ago. No matter what symptoms you had, the treatment would be the same.**

What is the meaning of *symptoms* as used in the sentence above?

Ⓐ ways to explain

Ⓑ signs of an illness

Ⓒ amounts of money

Ⓓ members of a family

22 Read this paragraph from the article.

> **One of the reasons so many people died was that doctors did not know about bacteria. They did not clean the germs from their hands or tools after working on one patient and beginning on another. Many patients got infections and died, but doctors did not understand why.**

Which details in the paragraph help the reader understand what *bacteria* means?

Ⓕ their hands or tools

Ⓖ one of the reasons

Ⓗ clean the germs

Ⓘ many patients

GO ON →

Name: ______________________________ Date: ________

23 Read this sentence from the article.

Barbers performed the same procedure on healthy people to help them stay healthy.

The root word for *procedure* is a Latin root meaning "go ahead." What does *procedure* mean?

Ⓐ beliefs

Ⓑ lesson

Ⓒ course of action

Ⓓ list of questions

24 With which of the following statements would the author most likely agree?

Ⓕ President Garfield might have survived if American doctors had used Joseph Lister's ideas.

Ⓖ Medical procedures probably will not change much in the future.

Ⓗ President Washington did not understand much about medicine.

Ⓘ Many years ago, bloodletting probably helped many people.

25 Which statement from the text expresses the author's viewpoint?

Ⓐ Many patients got infections and died, but doctors did not understand why.

Ⓑ One of the reasons so many people died was that doctors did not know about bacteria.

Ⓒ We are lucky that modern medicine is as advanced as it is and offers so many benefits.

Ⓓ A British surgeon, Joseph Lister, showed in 1867 that careful cleaning between patients could greatly reduce the risk of infections.

GO ON →

Name: ______________________ Date: ________

26. Explain why doctors long ago used bloodletting with patients. Use text evidence to support your answer.

____

____

____

____

____

____

27. According to evidence in the text, how are the doctors who worked on President Washington and modern doctors similar?

Ⓐ They use the best medical information available at the time.

Ⓑ They believe that a person can have too much "bad blood."

Ⓒ They understand that it's important to clean their tools.

Ⓓ They do not always do what the patient wants.

GO ON →

Name: ______________________________ Date: ________

28 The author organizes the structure of the paragraph about President Garfield by

Ⓕ showing how doctors lacked the tools to remove a bullet.

Ⓖ comparing and contrasting the surgeries of various presidents.

Ⓗ presenting the doctors' discussions about the president's condition.

Ⓘ showing that unclean surgical tools led to infection and the president's death.

29 In 1881, why were the doctors not able to save President Garfield?

Ⓐ The bullet had done too much damage.

Ⓑ The bullet could not be located.

Ⓒ Bloodletting led to the removal of too much blood.

Ⓓ The doctors' use of unclean tools caused an infection.

GO ON →

Name: ______________________________ Date: __________

30 Discuss how the practice of medicine changed in America after President Garfield's death. Use clear evidence from the text to support your position. How does the author organize his writing in order to present this historical information to the reader?

GO ON →

The passage below is a first draft that Audrey wrote. It contains mistakes. Read the passage to answer questions 31 through 40.

(1) I love going to visit my grandmother she lives in Charleston. (2) During our last visit, we went down to her basement where she keeps old pictures. (3) I found some other stuff that really surprised me. (4) It was almost like she had a museum in her basement!

(5) She doesn't always throw away old things when they get replaced. (6) One of the old things was a phone with a dial. (7) Every hole in the dial had a number and letters like on phone buttons now. (8) You had to stick your finger in the hole, and then you turned it around to dial a number. (9) I tried dialing a number, and it took most time than using buttons!

(10) I found a "boom box," too. (11) It was one of the first music players you could carry with you. (12) But it was worser than music players today. (13) It was as big as a suitcase, and it felt even heavier. (14) Grandma said that people bought the most big ones in the store so they could play their music louder.

(15) I'm glad I've got my modern cell phone and a small music player. (16) They are more good than the old machines. (17) With these devices, I don't have to dial numbers or carry a big suitcase around to hear my music.

GO ON →

Name: ______________________________ Date: ________

31 How can sentence 1 best be written?

Ⓐ I love going to visit my grandmother, she lives in Charleston.

Ⓑ I love going to visit my grandmother, lives in Charleston.

Ⓒ I love going to visit my grandmother who lives in Charleston.

Ⓓ I love going to visit my grandmother in Charleston, she lives there.

32 Which sentence uses a relative adverb to introduce a subordinate clause?

Ⓕ Sentence 2

Ⓖ Sentence 4

Ⓗ Sentence 7

Ⓘ Sentence 15

33 Which sentence has two independent clauses?

Ⓐ Sentence 5

Ⓑ Sentence 6

Ⓒ Sentence 7

Ⓓ Sentence 8

34 Which sentence contains a dependent clause?

Ⓕ Sentence 4

Ⓖ Sentence 5

Ⓗ Sentence 6

Ⓘ Sentence 7

GO ON →

Name: ______________________________ Date: ________

35 Which word in sentence 2 is an adjective that modifies a noun?

Ⓐ During
Ⓑ visit
Ⓒ down
Ⓓ old

36 How can sentence 9 best be written?

Ⓕ I tried dialing a number, and it took the most time than using buttons!

Ⓖ I tried dialing a number, and it took greatest time than using buttons!

Ⓗ I tried dialing a number, and it took morer time than using buttons!

Ⓘ I tried dialing a number, and it took more time than using buttons!

37 How can sentence 12 be written correctly?

Ⓐ But it was worst than music players today.

Ⓑ But it was more worse than music players today.

Ⓒ But it was worse than music players today.

Ⓓ But it was baddest than music players today.

38 How can sentence 14 be written correctly?

Ⓕ Grandma said that people bought the more bigger ones in the store so they could play their music louder.

Ⓖ Grandma said that people bought the biggest ones in the store so they could play their music louder.

Ⓗ Grandma said that people bought the most bigger ones in the store so they could play their music louder.

Ⓘ Grandma said that people bought the most biggest ones in the store so they could play their music louder.

GO ON →

Name: ______________________________ Date: __________

39 How can sentence 16 best be written?

Ⓐ They are better than the old machines.

Ⓑ They are gooder than the old machines.

Ⓒ They are more gooder than the old machines.

Ⓓ They are most good than the old machines.

40 Which word in sentence 17 is an adjective?

Ⓕ with

Ⓖ these

Ⓗ don't

Ⓘ around

STOP

Writing Prompt – Informative

Think of one important thing that has changed a lot during your life. For example, it might be communication, travel, or the types of activities you enjoy.

Write an informative essay telling about something that has changed, how it has changed, and how it has affected your life.

Use the space below to plan your writing. Write your final copy on a clean sheet of paper.

Answer Key Name: ______________________________

Question	Correct Answer	Content Focus	CCSS	Complexity
1	A	Root Words	L.5.4b	DOK 1
2	H	Context Clues: Comparison	L.5.4a	DOK 2
3	C	Idioms	L.5.5b	DOK 2
4	G	Greek Roots	L.5.4b	DOK 1
5	C	Literary Elements: Figurative Language	L.5.5c	DOK 2
6	I	Literary Elements: Narrator	RL.5.6	DOK 3
7	see below	Character, Setting, Plot: Compare and Contrast	RL.5.3	DOK 3
8	I	Character, Setting, Plot: Compare and Contrast	RL.5.3	DOK 2
9	C	Character, Setting, Plot: Compare and Contrast	RL.5.3	DOK 2
10	see below	Character, Setting, Plot: Compare and Contrast	RL.5.3	DOK 3
11	D	Idioms	L.5.5b	DOK 1
12	F	Context Clues: Comparison	L.5.4a	DOK 2
13	C	Text Features: Chart	RI.4.7	DOK 1
14	I	Context Clues: Paragraph Clues	L.5.4a	DOK 2
15	A	Literary Elements: Figurative Language	L.5.5a	DOK 2
16	H	Author's Point of View	RI.6.6	DOK 3
17	see below	Text Features: Chart	RI.4.7	DOK 3
18	I	Cause and Effect	RI.5.3	DOK 2
19	C	Author's Point of View	RI.5.8	DOK 3
20	see below	Compare Across Texts	W.5.9	DOK 4
21	B	Context Clues: Comparison	L.5.4a	DOK 2
22	H	Context Clues: Paragraph Clues	L.5.4a	DOK 2

Answer Key

Name: ____________________

Question	Correct Answer	Content Focus	CCSS	Complexity
23	C	Root Words	L.5.4b	DOK 1
24	F	Author's Point of View	RI.6.6	DOK 3
25	C	Author's Point of View	RI.6.6	DOK 3
26	see below	Cause and Effect	RI.5.3	DOK 2
27	A	Text Structure: Compare and Contrast	RI.5.3	DOK 2
28	I	Text Structure: Cause and Effect	RI.5.3	DOK 3
29	D	Cause and Effect	RI.5.3	DOK 2
30	see below	Text Structure: Cause and Effect	RI.5.3	DOK 3
31	C	Complex Sentences	L.5.1	DOK 1
32	F	Complex Sentences	L.5.1	DOK 1
33	D	Independent and Dependent Clauses	L.5.1	DOK 1
34	G	Independent and Dependent Clauses	L.5.1	DOK 1
35	D	Adjectives	L.5.1	DOK 1
36	I	Adjectives That Compare	L.5.1	DOK 1
37	C	Comparing with Good and Bad	L.5.1	DOK 1
38	G	Adjectives That Compare	L.5.1	DOK 1
39	A	Comparing with Good and Bad	L.5.1	DOK 1
40	G	Adjectives	L.5.1	DOK 1
Prompt	see below	Informative Writing	W.5.2a-e	DOK 3

Comprehension: Multiple-Choice 5, 6, 8, 9, 13, 15, 16, 18, 19, 24, 25, 27, 28, 29	/14	%
Comprehension: Constructed Responses 7, 10, 17, 20, 26, 30	/16	%
Vocabulary 1, 2, 3, 4, 11, 12, 14, 21, 22, 23	/10	%
Grammar, Mechanics, Usage 31-40	/10	%
Total Unit Assessment Score	/50	%

Answer Key   Name: ______________________

7 **2-point item.** Tranh and Karen are like the other students in that they are excited about going into the cave and want to see everything. They are different because they break the rules by trying to go into the cave early.

10 **2-point item.** Student response should note that the students are like real spelunkers because they explore a dark cave and have fun. They are different because they are exploring as students on a field trip, not for a hobby, and they are expected to learn about caves in the process.

17 **2-point item.** The Wild Cave tour is the most difficult. It lasts 6 hours, covers 5 miles, and involves crawling through caves. The Mammoth Passage tour is easiest. It lasts only 1 ¼ hours and goes ¾ mile through the largest rooms.

20 **4-point item.** Students should note that the early explorers of Mammoth Cave had only simple equipment, such as candles and a ladder, while the class trip was prepared with flashlights, helmets, and scientific equipment, such as thermometers. The early explorers had to take many chances to explore new passages while the school trip was visiting an area well-known to the teachers. The early explorers loved the cave and became very knowledgeable about the geology. Two were also able to purchase their freedom. Exploring on the class trip would add to the students' scientific knowledge and might inspire them to learn more about caves or related scientific subjects.

26 **2-point item.** Doctors believed that the human body held four humors, and those humors had to be balanced. Blood was one of the humors. A person who got sick had too much "bad blood," so it had to be removed to heal the patient.

30 **4-point item.** Students should explain that Garfield died from infection rather than from his bullet wound. The surgeons working on him did not clean their tools. Garfield's death convinced American doctors that Lister was right about bacteria and the need for sterile procedures, and they changed their procedures after that. The author has organized the structure of his text by cause and effect.

Writing Prompt

Refer to the scoring criteria in the Teacher Introduction to assess written responses to the prompt.

Read the article and the passage. Then answer the questions that follow.

Amelia Earhart: Pioneer

Amelia Earhart was born in 1897 in a small Kansas town. That was six years before the Wright brothers took their famous first airplane flight in Kitty Hawk, North Carolina. Over the next two decades, aviation developed rapidly. The pilots at the controls were mainly men. Amelia Earhart broke through that barrier to become a famous aviator, and she paved the way for the women who followed.

Early Life

Amelia's early life was spent in many Midwestern towns. Her father had difficulty keeping a job. At times, Amelia lived with her grandparents. Her family moved frequently so her father could search for new employment. As a result, Amelia attended many different schools. She had trouble making friends and earning good grades, even though she was very bright.

The first time Amelia saw an airplane she was 12 years old, but it wasn't until several years later that she felt the urge to lift off. After graduating from high school, she worked as a nurse's aide and took care of wounded soldiers returning from World War I. Many of her patients were pilots. By talking with them, she became more interested in aviation.

In December 1920, Amelia attended the Long Beach Air Show in California. At the air show, she rode as a passenger on a 10-minute airplane flight. It was an experience that forever changed her life. As soon as she left the ground, Amelia knew she had to learn to fly.

Amelia Takes Off

Amelia took her first flying lesson in 1921. At the end of the year, she received her pilot's license. She took odd jobs and received financial help from her mother to buy her own airplane.

GO ON →

Amelia quickly began making a name for herself in the aviation world. In October 1922, she broke a world record for female pilots by flying her plane to 14,000 feet in altitude. In 1923, she received her International Pilot's License—just the sixteenth woman in the world to do so. Unfortunately, Amelia had to sell her plane to give her mother money. For a while, her love of aviation became more of a hobby.

But this all changed in 1928 when Amelia was contacted by publisher George Putnam, whom she later married. He invited her to be a passenger on a cross-Atlantic flight. Amelia would have preferred to be the pilot, not the passenger. But at the time, flying a plane over an ocean was considered too dangerous for women.

The flight was successful, and Amelia became world-famous as the first woman to fly across the Atlantic. However, Amelia wasn't satisfied. She didn't get to operate the controls during the flight and thought of herself to be no more important to the flight's success than "a sack of potatoes." She was determined to fly on her own.

Amelia Reaches Stardom

In 1929, Amelia became involved with an organization called the Ninety-Nines, a group that promoted female pilots in the aviation industry. She was the group's first president. In May of 1932, Amelia crossed the Atlantic again, but this time she was at the controls. She made the trip from Canada to Ireland in 15 hours. She received many medals and awards for her achievement.

Amelia hoped her success would open doors for women in aviation and in other fields, so she continued flying and setting records. She became the first person to fly across both the Atlantic and Pacific oceans when she flew from Hawaii to California.

An Extraordinary Mission

Even after proving she was a world-class aviator, Amelia still wanted more. In 1937, she set off on an amazing trip: flying around the world. Amelia started in California but faced trouble along the way. She became ill; her plane needed repairs; and bad weather forced a change in the flight route. She made it to one of her planned stops near Australia, but she never made it to her next destination.

GO ON →

People all over the world were following the news of Amelia's trip—and now she was missing! President Franklin D. Roosevelt conducted a $4 million rescue mission, but Amelia was never found.

Amelia hoped that her actions would inspire other women to follow their dreams. One of her lifelong missions was for the world to recognize that women could have the same careers as men. Even though she died at a young age, just 40 years old, Amelia was an inspiration to many.

GO ON →

A Basketball Dream

"How many points are you going to score today?" my friend Jesse asks as I wrap my leg with an elastic bandage.

"I'm hoping for at least 20. You?" I reply as I finish wrapping. Then Jesse and I join the team for practice at the end of the court.

My leg isn't wrapped because of an injury. I wrap it every game to make sure I don't injure other people! This may sound strange, but let me explain. I was born without a tibia in my right leg (your tibia is the shin bone below your knee). When I was just two years old, I got a prosthetic leg. It's made of metal and plastic, which is why I have to wrap it in case another player runs into me. If you didn't know I had a fake leg, you probably wouldn't be able to tell. At first, my parents and friends thought it would be too difficult for me to play, but they soon found out I can play just as well as anyone!

I've been playing basketball all my life. When I was three, my father placed a small plastic hoop on the back of my door. Every day, I took practice shots with an orange foam ball. As I got older, my parents installed a real hoop in our driveway. I practiced every day after school. All of my hard work paid off because I made the Ridgemont Middle School basketball team as a sixth grader. I've never let my leg stop me from reaching my goals. I've had to work hard to learn how to run and jump, but I never gave up.

After sinking a practice shot from the three-point line, I hear Coach Sanders blow the whistle, so I run over to the bench.

"Jason, watch number 45's outside shot," he tells me. "He scored 30 points last game, so we may have to double-team him."

"Got it, Coach," I reply. Coach Sanders issues a few more commands to the starting players, and then the referee's whistle blows. It's game time.

I remember the first time I stepped onto the basketball court to play in my first game. My head was swimming with the sounds of cheering fans. I didn't think I'd be nervous, but I was.

GO ON →

I then realized that this was going to be very different from playing in the driveway with my dad! When my teammate won the tip-off, the orange orb headed straight for me. I caught it but felt like I was frozen in place. I soon came back to reality, turned, and headed down the court, the sound of the bouncing ball echoed in my ears.

From that moment on, my playing improved. Every game I got better and better. I sprinted up and down the court, keeping up with the other players. The ball was like a streak of lightning as I passed it across the court. The net seemed to nod its head with approval after almost every shot I took.

Sometimes I get very tired, and the ball feels like lead in my hands, but I don't let it defeat me. I push as hard as I can, knowing that I can rest later.

Today is a special day because my grandmother is in the stands for the very first time. She moved to Florida last year, so she has never seen me play on my new team. I call her after every game to tell her about how many points I scored or how many shots I blocked. Today, she'll get to see for herself.

I take my position on the court and get ready for tip-off. I keep a close eye on number 45, just as Coach told me to do. I can tell he's a good player by the way he dribbles the ball effortlessly between his legs. Suddenly, he takes a shot. I leap into the air and swat away the ball, blocking his shot! My teammate Tommy grabs the ball, runs down the court, and takes an easy shot to score the first points of the game. When I look up at the stands and see my grandmother beaming with pride, that makes my game even better.

GO ON →

Name: ________________________________ Date: __________

Use "Amelia Earhart: Pioneer" on pages 137–139 to answer Numbers 1 through 10.

1 Read the first paragraph of the article. Which words from the paragraph help the reader understand what *aviator* means?

Ⓐ a small Kansas town

Ⓑ the next two decades

Ⓒ pilots at the controls

Ⓓ for the women who followed

2 Read these sentences from the article.

She made the trip from Canada to Ireland in 15 hours. She received many medals and awards for her achievement.

The author uses *achievement* instead of *deed* to suggest that the trip

Ⓕ was an ordinary one.

Ⓖ was almost unsuccessful.

Ⓗ required ability and great effort.

Ⓘ meant that Amelia had nothing left to accomplish.

3 What problems did Amelia face during her childhood? Use text evidence from the article to support your answer.

____

____

____

____

____

____

GO ON →

Name: ______________________________ Date: ________

4 Read this sentence from the article.

At the air show, she rode as a passenger on a 10-minute airplane flight.

Which definition fits *rode* as it is used in the sentence above?

Ⓕ way to go

Ⓖ took a ride

Ⓗ paddled with oars

Ⓘ strip of pavement or ground for vehicles

5 Why did Amelia sell her plane?

Ⓐ Her mother needed money.

Ⓑ Her father could not find a job.

Ⓒ She had to live with her grandparents.

Ⓓ She decided flying should be just a hobby.

6 Which word is a homophone for the word defined below?

to see how heavy something is

Ⓕ aide

Ⓖ field

Ⓗ way

Ⓘ world

7 After her first cross-Atlantic flight, why did Amelia say that she was no more important than a "sack of potatoes"?

Ⓐ She did not have the skills required to be a pilot.

Ⓑ She did not get to operate the controls during the flight.

Ⓒ She thought she had stopped the flight from being a success.

Ⓓ She wanted to show that she was satisfied with the experience.

GO ON →

Name: ______________________________ Date: ______

8 Read this sentence from the article.

President Franklin D. Roosevelt conducted a $4 million rescue mission, but Amelia was never found.

Which word has almost the same meaning as *conducted* as used in the sentence above?

Ⓕ considered

Ⓖ canceled

Ⓗ directed

Ⓘ followed

9 Why does the author include details about Amelia's work as a nurse's aide?

Ⓐ to tell the complete sequence of events in her life

Ⓑ to show what caused her interest in becoming a pilot

Ⓒ to describe how she solved a problem by helping others

Ⓓ to explain how being a nurse is different from being a pilot

10 What problems did Amelia face once she decided she wanted to become a pilot, and how did she solve those problems? Support your answer with clear text evidence.

____

____

____

____

____

____

GO ON →

Name: ______________________________ Date: __________

Use "A Basketball Dream" on pages 140 and 141 to answer Numbers 11 through 20.

11 Which sentence shows that Jason is determined?

Ⓐ I wrap it every game to make sure I don't injure other people!

Ⓑ I've had to work hard to learn how to run and jump, but I never gave up.

Ⓒ I call her after every game to tell her about how many points I scored or how many shots I blocked.

Ⓓ I then realized that this was going to be very different from playing in the driveway with my dad!

12 Read this sentence from the passage.

The net seemed to nod its head with approval after almost every shot I took.

The author compares the net to a person nodding to show that

Ⓕ Jason needs a lot of practice.

Ⓖ Jason is making a lot of his shots.

Ⓗ the net seems large.

Ⓘ the net is broken.

13 What important information does the author tell readers near the end of the passage?

Ⓐ Jason was born without part of his leg.

Ⓑ Jason's grandmother is watching him play.

Ⓒ Jason made the middle school basketball team as a sixth grader.

Ⓓ Jason's parents got him interested in basketball when he was young.

GO ON →

Name: ______________________________ Date: ________

14 What is the theme in this passage?

Ⓕ Hard work pays off.

Ⓖ Respect your elders.

Ⓗ Good friends are important in life.

Ⓘ Get to know people before you judge them.

15 How does the narrator in this passage feel about his grandmother? Use text evidence from the passage in your answer.

____

____

____

____

____

____

16 Which evidence from the text tells you that Jason is proud of his achievements?

Ⓕ He wraps his leg with an elastic bandage.

Ⓖ He calls his grandmother after every game.

Ⓗ He listens closely to his coach's instructions.

Ⓘ He has been playing basketball since he was young.

GO ON →

Name: ______________________________ Date: __________

17 Which descriptive detail from the passage tells about how Jason moves?

Ⓐ I take my position on the court and get ready for tip-off.

Ⓑ My head was swimming with the sounds of cheering fans.

Ⓒ I sprinted up and down the court, keeping up with the other players.

Ⓓ I've never let my leg stop me from reaching my goals.

18 Identify a flashback found in this passage. Then explain why the flashback you have identified is important to the passage. Support your answer with clear text evidence.

____

____

____

____

____

____

19 Read this sentence from the passage.

Sometimes I get very tired, and the ball feels like lead in my hands, but I don't let it defeat me.

The descriptive details in this sentence support the idea that Jason

Ⓐ is determined.

Ⓑ is a skillful player.

Ⓒ tries hard to do what the coach wants.

Ⓓ gets tired more easily than other players.

GO ON →

Name: ______________________________ Date: ________

Use “Amelia Earhart: Pioneer” and “A Basketball Dream” to answer the question below.

20 Amelia Earhart and Jason both faced challenges in reaching their goals. Explain how their experiences were similar and what those experiences teach people about achieving their goals. Use text evidence from the article and the passage to support your response.

GO ON →

Read the letter to the editor before answering Numbers 21 through 30.

A Letter to the Editor

To the editor of *Oliver Community News*:

I would like readers of this newspaper to know about a special event. It is the yearly art show of the Pen and Ink Club at Oliver High School. Most people haven't heard the phrase "pen and ink drawing." However, they have probably seen at least one such drawing in their lifetime, in a book or hanging on a wall. Pen and ink drawing is just like pencil drawing. Yet it is a little trickier to learn. The most difficult part of learning it is the fact that ink is permanent. The artist cannot make a mistake because this ink cannot be erased.

Here are some details about the upcoming show. It is titled "Creatures in Ink." The opening is on Friday, November 2, at 6:30 P.M. in the Oliver Community Center next door to the high school. The drawings will remain on exhibit for three weeks after the opening.

In my opinion, "Creatures in Ink" is the best art show our club has ever held. Everyone who has already seen the drawings agrees with me. These drawings leap off the paper and grab you by the collar.

Many people have said that there are more talented students this year than usual. The proof of that talent is how many beautiful drawings there are in the show. A reporter for our school newspaper interviewed our principal about the Pen and Ink Club and the upcoming show. She told the reporter that she was proud to be part of a school with such gifted students.

Finally, Javier Ramos, a former student of Oliver High, came to see the drawings as they were being prepared for the show. Mr. Ramos is a now a famous artist. He commented that the work was incredible. He said that when he was in high school, his drawings were not nearly as good. In fact, he said that his drawing skills at that time were rudimentary compared to what he saw here.

GO ON →

In the show, you'll see ink drawings of dinosaurs, birds, lizards, spiders, and monkeys. All of the drawings look very realistic. Every drawing took weeks, maybe months, to create. When you go to the show, plan to use your skills as a careful observer. Be sure to spend time in front of each drawing so you can appreciate the details.

Several people who have seen the drawings have said that the Pen and Ink Club should be given a special prize. I'm confident that by the time the exhibit is over, the entire community will love "Creatures in Ink." It is almost guaranteed that no one will leave the show disappointed.

Andrew Warrel

Secretary, Pen and Ink Club

Pen and ink drawing is not for everyone, but artists who choose to work with ink say that it is worth all the trouble. They like it because they can create pictures that are very exact.

GO ON →

Name: ______________________________ Date: ________

Now answer Numbers 21 through 30. Base your answers on "A Letter to the Editor."

21 What makes pen and ink drawing trickier than other types of drawing?

Ⓐ It is easier to make mistakes.

Ⓑ The drawings cannot be erased.

Ⓒ The ink is difficult to use on paper.

Ⓓ It takes a long time to learn how to do it.

22 Which pair of words from the letter have almost the same meaning?

Ⓕ incredible, good

Ⓖ talented, gifted

Ⓗ confident, careful

Ⓘ beautiful, realistic

23 Read this sentence from the letter.

> **These drawings leap off the paper and grab you by the collar.**

What does this sentence mean?

Ⓐ Nobody can keep these drawings up on the wall.

Ⓑ These drawings jump on your shirt and hold onto your collar.

Ⓒ The drawings leave ink stains on your collar if you grab them.

Ⓓ These drawings are so good that they really get your attention.

GO ON →

Name: ______________________________ Date: ________

24 The illustration best supports which idea in the letter?

Ⓕ The drawings took weeks or months to create.

Ⓖ All of the drawings in the exhibit look realistic.

Ⓗ The Pen and Ink Club deserves a special prize for the exhibit.

Ⓘ There are an unusually large number of talented students in the Pen and Ink Club.

25 Which detail best supports the idea that "Creatures in Ink" is the best art show the club has ever held?

Ⓐ A reporter from the school newspaper interviewed the principal.

Ⓑ The show will contain drawings of many types of animals.

Ⓒ Every drawing took the artist a long time to create.

Ⓓ Javier Ramos said the work was incredible.

26 Read these sentences from the letter.

He said that when he was in high school, his drawings were not nearly as good. In fact, he said that his drawing skills at that time were rudimentary compared to what he saw here.

What does *rudimentary* mean in the sentences above?

Ⓕ boring

Ⓖ clever

Ⓗ educated

Ⓘ undeveloped

GO ON →

Name: ______________________________ Date: ________

27 Read this sentence from the letter.

Every drawing took weeks, maybe months, to create.

Which word has the OPPOSITE meaning of the word *create*?

Ⓐ appreciate

Ⓑ destroy

Ⓒ invent

Ⓓ produce

28 Why does the writer speak directly to the reader and tell them to use their "skills as a careful observer" when they go to the show?

Ⓕ to challenge them to look for mistakes in the drawings

Ⓖ to explain how pen and pencil drawings are different

Ⓗ to tell that the drawings will be judged for a prize

Ⓘ to encourage them to attend the show

29 Read this sentence from the letter.

It is almost guaranteed that no one will leave the show disappointed.

What does the writer suggest is the reason that no one will leave disappointed?

Ⓐ They will be impressed by the number of drawings.

Ⓑ They will be delighted by the quality of the drawings.

Ⓒ They will find that the drawings are truly of creatures.

Ⓓ They will never have seen drawings of these creatures before.

GO ON →

Name: ______________________________ Date: __________

30 What problems does the author of the letter seem to have in making the art show sound appealing, and how does he try to solve those problems? Use details from the letter to explain your answer.

GO ON →

This is a draft of the first part of a passage that Millie wrote. It contains mistakes. Read this part of the passage to answer questions 31 through 35.

(1) Elizabeth sat in the kitchen and washed her father's soiled shirt. (2) She rubbed it against the washboard back and forth that was set in the basin. (3) The water quickly turned brown as Elizabeth washed the mud away. (4) Suddenly, Elizabeth heard her parents' voices in the next room. (5) She stopped rubbing the shirt and listened closer.

(6) "William, I'm going to the sit-in tomorrow," said her mother. (7) "Women should have a right to vote in this town."

(8) "Victoria, of course I agree with you," her father said. (9) "But I'm worried that the protesters will be arrested!"

(10) Elizabeth's mother answered firmly. (11) "I'm sorry, but you can't never change my mind. (12) I'm going to the town hall. (13) I will be there at 8 A.M. tomorrow."

(14) "I wish you didn't have to do this, but I understand your reasons," said Father.

(15) Elizabeth could hear him walking. (16) He was coming toward the kitchen.

GO ON →

Name: ______________________________ Date: ________

31 How can sentence 2 best be written?

Ⓐ Against the washboard that was set in the basin back and forth she rubbed it.

Ⓑ Rubbed it against the washboard that was set in the basin back and forth she did.

Ⓒ She rubbed it against the washboard that was set in the basin back and forth.

Ⓓ She rubbed it back and forth against the washboard that was set in the basin.

32 How can sentence 5 be written correctly?

Ⓕ She stopped rubbing the shirt and listened most close.

Ⓖ She stopped rubbing the shirt and listened more close.

Ⓗ She stopped rubbing the shirt and listened most closest.

Ⓘ She stopped rubbing the shirt and listened more closely.

33 How can sentence 11 best be written?

Ⓐ "I'm sorry, but you can't change my mind."

Ⓑ "I'm sorry, but you can't not ever change my mind."

Ⓒ "I'm sorry, but you cannot never change my mind."

Ⓓ "I'm sorry, but you can't hardly change my mind."

GO ON →

Name: ______________________________ Date: ________

34 How can sentences 12 and 13 best be combined?

Ⓕ "I will be at the town hall at 8 A.M. tomorrow."

Ⓖ "Tomorrow, I'm going to the town hall at 8 A.M., I will be there."

Ⓗ "I'm going to the town hall, I will be there at 8 A.M. tomorrow."

Ⓘ "Because I'm going to the town hall, I will be there at 8 A.M. tomorrow."

35 Which revision best combines sentences 15 and 16?

Ⓐ Elizabeth could hear him toward the kitchen walking.

Ⓑ Elizabeth could hear him walking toward the kitchen.

Ⓒ Elizabeth could hear him walking and he was coming toward the kitchen.

Ⓓ Elizabeth could hear him toward the kitchen coming and walking.

GO ON →

Read the next part of the story. Choose the word or words that correctly complete questions 36–40.

Elizabeth's father came ___(36)___ and poured himself a drink of water. Elizabeth didn't want to let him know she had been listening to his conversation, but she couldn't help herself. "Father, why ___(37)___ Mother be able to vote?" she asked.

He looked at her ___(38)___ for a moment and then pulled up a chair next to the washbasin. "Well, some men in the town think that men should be the only people allowed to vote. What do you think about that?"

Elizabeth sat up straight and crossed her arms. "I don't think that's right. Women should be treated ___(39)___, and we should have the same rights as men," she stated.

"Unfortunately, not everyone thinks that way. But I have a feeling that your mother is going to change that ___(40)___ she gets to the town hall tomorrow," he said. Then his eyes lit up, and he smiled. "In fact, I think I'll go down there and sit with her."

GO ON →

Name: ______________________________ Date: ________

36 Which answer should go in blank (36)?

Ⓕ the kitchen

Ⓖ into the kitchen

Ⓗ after the kitchen

37 Which answer should go in blank (37)?

Ⓐ shouldn't not

Ⓑ shouldn't never

Ⓒ shouldn't

38 Which answer should go in blank (38)?

Ⓕ thoughtful

Ⓖ thoughtfully

Ⓗ more thoughtful

39 Which answer should go in blank (39)?

Ⓐ more fair

Ⓑ fairer

Ⓒ more fairly

40 Which answer should go in blank (40)?

Ⓕ when

Ⓖ so

Ⓗ although

STOP

Writing Prompt – Opinion Piece

Suppose a principal at an elementary school is considering making students wear school uniforms. Some students agree with the idea, and other students are against it.

Write an opinion piece that states your opinion about school uniforms. Be sure to include reasons and ideas that support your view.

Use the space below to plan your writing. Write your opinion piece on a clean sheet of paper.

Answer Key

Name: ______________________________

Question	Correct Answer	Content Focus	CCSS	Complexity
1	C	Context Clues: Paragraph Clues	L.5.4a	DOK 2
2	H	Connotation and Denotation	L.5.5	DOK 2
3	see below	Problem and Solution	RI.5.3	DOK 2
4	G	Homophones	L.5.4	DOK 1
5	A	Cause and Effect	RI.5.3	DOK 2
6	H	Homophones	L.5.4	DOK 1
7	B	Cause and Effect	RI.5.3	DOK 2
8	H	Synonyms	L.5.5c	DOK 2
9	B	Text Structure: Cause and Effect	RI.5.3	DOK 2
10	see below	Problem and Solution	RI.5.5	DOK 2
11	B	Literary Element: Point of View	RL.5.6	DOK 3
12	G	Personification	L.5.5a	DOK 2
13	B	Literary Element: Pacing	RL.5.5	DOK 1
14	F	Theme	RL.5.2	DOK 3
15	see below	Literary Element: Point of View	RL.5.6	DOK 3
16	G	Literary Element: Point of View	RL.5.6	DOK 3
17	C	Literary Element: Descriptive Details	RL.5.4	DOK 2
18	see below	Literary Element: Flashback	RL.5.5	DOK 3
19	A	Literary Element: Descriptive Details	RL.5.4	DOK 2
20	see below	Compare Across Texts	W.5.9	DOK 4
21	B	Problem and Solution	RI.5.3	DOK 2
22	G	Synonyms	L.5.5c	DOK 1

Answer Key

Name: ______________________

Question	Correct Answer	Content Focus	CCSS	Complexity
23	D	Personification	L.5.5a	DOK 2
24	G	Use Illustrations	RI.4.7	DOK 2
25	D	Main Idea and Key Details	RI.5.2	DOK 2
26	I	Context Clues: Paragraph Clues	L.5.4a	DOK 2
27	B	Antonyms	L.5.5c	DOK 2
28	I	Text Structure: Cause and Effect	RI.5.3	DOK 2
29	B	Cause and Effect	RI.5.3	DOK 2
30	see below	Text Structure: Problem and Solution	RI.5.5	DOK 2
31	D	Prepositional Phrases as Adjectives and Adverbs	L.5.1a	DOK 2
32	I	Adverbs that Compare	L.5.1	DOK 1
33	A	Negatives	L.5.1	DOK 1
34	F	Sentence Combining	L.5.1	DOK 1
35	B	Sentence Combining	L.5.1	DOK 1
36	G	Prepositional Phrases as Adjectives and Adverbs	L.5.1a	DOK 1
37	C	Negatives	L.5.1	DOK 1
38	G	Adverbs	L.5.1	DOK 1
39	C	Adverbs that Compare	L.5.1	DOK 1
40	F	Adverbs	L.5.1	DOK 1
Prompt	see below	Opinion Writing	W.5.1a-d	DOK 3

Comprehension: Multiple-Choice 5, 7, 9, 11, 13, 14, 16, 17, 19, 21, 24, 25, 28, 29	/14	%
Comprehension: Constructed Response 3, 10, 15, 18, 20, 30	/16	%
Vocabulary 1, 2, 4, 6, 8, 12, 22, 23, 26, 27	/10	%
Grammar, Mechanics, Usage 31–40	/10	%
Total Unit Assessment Score	/50	%

 Name: ___________________________

3 **2-point item.** The response should indicate that Amelia's father could not keep a job, so the family moved around a lot. Amelia had trouble making friends and did not do well in school.

10 **2-point item.** Most pilots were men, and women had few opportunities to learn to fly. When Amelia became a pilot, people thought it was too dangerous for women to do really long flights. They didn't think women should fly planes as a career. She also had to sell her plane to give her mother money, so flying became a hobby for a while.

15 **2-point item.** The response should note that Jason clearly loves his grandmother and wants her to be impressed with his play. This is "a special day" because Grandma will be in the stands.

18 **2-point item.** In one flashback, Jason remembers playing in his first basketball game. He felt nervous because it was different from playing in his driveway. He felt frozen when he got the ball, but soon he snapped out of it and played well. This is important because it shows how well he adjusted to playing in a real game. In another flashback, he thinks back to playing basketball as a toddler with the foam ball and later in his driveway. This flashback is important because it reveals how long basketball has interested him and gives several reasons for why he might be so good at it.

20 **4-point item.** The response should be in paragraph form. Amelia Earhart wanted to fly across the ocean and around the world, but people thought women were unable to fly such distances safely. Jason wanted to play basketball, but his friends and family doubted him at first. They did not think a person with a prosthetic leg could or should try to play basketball. Both Amelia Earhart's and Jason's experiences teach people to fight for what they want and not give up on their dreams.

30 **4-point item.** The response should be in paragraph form. Students should explain that the author realizes people may not know what pen and ink drawing is, and they may not think that high school students are talented enough to create truly good artwork. He tries to solve these problems by explaining pen and ink drawing. Then he praises the quality of the artwork and gives evidence to support his view, including statements from the principal and from a well-known artist, Javier Ramos.

Writing Prompt

Refer to the scoring criteria in the Teacher Introduction to assess written responses to the prompt.